Your
TAROT
Guide

Your
TAROT
Guide

Learn to navigate life with the help of the cards

MELINDA LEE HOLM

Illustrations by **Rohan Daniel Eason**

CICO BOOKS
LONDON NEW YORK

Dedicated to the late great Rachel Pollack.

Published in 2023 by CICO Books
An imprint of Ryland Peters & Small Ltd
20–21 Jockey's Fields   341 E 116th St
London WC1R 4BW   New York, NY 10029

www.rylandpeters.com

10 9 8 7 6 5 4 3 2 1

A CIP catalog record for this book is available from
the Library of Congress and the British Library.

ISBN: 978 1 80065 260 6

Printed in China

Designer: Geoff Borin
Illustrator: Rohan Daniel Eason

Commissioning editor: Kristine Pidkameny
In-house editor: Jenny Dye
Art director: Sally Powell
Creative director: Leslie Harrington
Head of production: Patricia Harrington
Publishing manager: Penny Craig

Contents

Introduction

Welcome to *Your Tarot Guide*! Within these pages you will find everything you need to begin navigating life using tarot as your compass. Tarot found me when I needed it most. It was my light in the darkness when I was a troubled 15-year-old and it is the trusted friend I turn to for guidance now, 30 years later.

Tarot is a language and a tool. With practice, you'll gain fluency and find your voice, enabling you to create and read your own maps and fables to guide you through big transitions, help focus your energy where it will be most useful, and understand and love yourself more deeply and profoundly than you thought possible. When tarot is used in this way, there is nothing to be afraid of. There are no "bad" cards, there is only information and conversation. Tarot cannot tell you what will happen in your life. It offers something much more valuable: a way to navigate toward the life you dream of.

While the information in *Your Tarot Guide* is applicable to any tarot deck, the cards shown in this book are from my two tarot decks, *Elemental Power Tarot* and *Tarot of Tales*.

Elemental Power Tarot (see cards from this deck below) is an intellectual approach to tarot and its system of archetypes, elements, and numerology. The Major Arcana cards show scenes full of symbols that reflect the qualities of the card archetypes*, and are invitations to step into these roles.

The Minor Arcana cards of *Elemental Power Tarot* focus on the classical element of each suit (Cups/Water, Swords/Air, Wands/Fire, Coins/Earth). The numbered cards have backgrounds that reflect their elements as well as suit symbols arranged in formations to evoke the meaning of each card, while the court cards (see page 16)

I THE MAGICIAN

...T OF SWORDS

...OF COINS

combine elemental energies with various "hats" for the reader to wear to become the Pages, Knights, Queens, and Kings.

Tarot of Tales (see cards from this deck above) is a storybook-themed deck with an experiential approach to tarot. Each card is a glimpse into a fairy tale world created in collaboration with illustrator Rohan Daniel Eason (illustrator of *Elemental Power Tarot*, *Your Magickal Year*, *Tarot of Tales*, and *Your Tarot Guide*). In this deck, the suits are presented as realms: Cups/Realm of Water, Swords/Realm of Air, Wands/Realm of Fire, and Coins/Realm of Earth. The creatures of these realms engage in activities representative of their card that show how it feels to live in the energy of that card. The cards and the guidebook present tarot readings as personal folk tales, and encourage you to choose your own adventure to continue the story.

Both decks were designed without human figures because I believe that tarot is for everyone. My hope is that by eliminating a specific human presence, everyone can see themself reflected in the cards.

I am wishing you the best on your tarot journey and your journey through life. Remember, tarot shows a map, but you steer the boat.

Bon voyage!

Melinda

Archetypes are figures that appear in mythological and storytelling traditions throughout the world and are known for their singular role and purpose. For example, the archetype of The Empress that we see in tarot only represents qualities of The Empress (creating abundance through nurturing), while an actual empress would have many other qualities that make up a whole human being.

CHAPTER 1

The Basics

The first step on your path to tarot mastery is understanding where tarot comes from and what makes it special. In this section you will learn what makes a deck of cards a tarot deck, how the deck functions as a whole, and best practices for choosing and caring for your deck. There are also some exercises to help you get better acquainted with your new best friend. Plus, there are exercises to help you get better acquainted with the cards and answers to the questions I get asked most frequently about reading tarot.

What is a Tarot Deck?

Tarot decks are decks of cards that follow a specific format and are used for game play or to access information through magickal* or spiritual means. We are focusing on the latter purpose. They contain 78 cards as follows:

✦ 22 Major Arcana cards, numbered 0–21.
✦ 56 Minor Arcana cards divided into four suits: Swords, Wands, Cups, and Coins or Pentacles. Each of these suits has ten cards numbered Ace–10 and four court cards: Page, Knight, Queen, and King.

I use magick spelled with a "k" at the end to refer to any practice that draws on the powers of the Earth, the Elements, and/or the Universe to bring about change and clarity in one's life.

The Major Arcana cards from *Tarot of Tales*

0 THE FOOL · I THE MAGICIAN

II THE HIGH PRIESTESS · III THE EMPRESS

IV THE EMPEROR · V THE HIEROPHANT · VI THE LOVERS · VII THE CHARIOT · VIII STRENGTH · IX THE HERMIT

X THE WHEEL OF FORTUNE · XI JUSTICE · XII THE HANGED MAN · XIII DEATH · XIV TEMPERANCE · XV THE DEVIL

XVI THE TOWER · XVII THE STAR · XVIII THE MOON · XIX THE SUN · XX JUDGMENT · XXI THE WORLD

The Minor Arcana cards from *Tarot of Tales*

The suit of Swords

The suit of Wands

The suit of Cups

The suit of Coins

Some decks have different names for the cards and a few add an extra Major Arcana card or two, but this is the basic structure of all tarot decks.

Many decks of cards are used for magickal and spiritual purposes. If they follow the format above, we call them tarot decks. If they do not, we generally call them oracle decks unless they prefer to be called something else, in which case we respect their wishes.

The Origins of Tarot

While the earliest tarot cards date from fifteenth-century Italy, there is no record of the cards being used for anything other than game play until the eighteenth century. In 1781, Antoine Court de Gébelin published the first esoteric meanings associated with the cards. He also claimed the cards contained a secret embedded book of ancient Egyptian wisdom, an idea that continues to this day though there is no historical evidence to support this theory.

The figures and archetypes depicted on the cards draw from life in southern Europe at the time, which was dominated by the

Sixteenth-century French tarot card designs for The Pope (above) and The Popess (right) next to their modern-day equivalents from *Tarot of Tales*: The Hierophant and The High Priestess.

Catholic church. This is why early decks refer to The Hierophant as The Pope and The High Priestess as The Popess. Other figures from early medieval mystery plays (which were Bible-based) and morality plays (which depicted a general struggle between good and evil) appear in the Major Arcana: The Fool, Death, Temperance, The Moon, and more. Though the early decks present these figures through a Christian lens, the archetypes themselves predate Christianity, which is one reason tarot remains relevant across belief systems and traditions today.

In the late nineteenth century, The Hermetic Order of the Golden Dawn, a magickal society based in London, organized, developed, and systematized many forms of magickal practice including tarot. The astrological and Qabbalistic associations commonly attributed to the cards come from their work.

Today, many tarot readers work to frame the original teachings of tarot in a way that is relevant to modern life and inclusive to the vast diversity of people who use the tarot to find focus, guidance, and wisdom. This is the intention of *Your Tarot Guide*.

Whoever you are and wherever you come from, tarot, and this book, are for you.

LA·PAPESSE

II THE HIGH PRIESTESS

Parts of the Deck

Major Arcana

The 22 cards of the Major Arcana represent archetypes with roots across cultures worldwide that we embody and encounter throughout life. These cards speak to inner evolution, life phases, and themes—ways of being more than ways of doing.

In the late nineteenth century, the Hermetic Order of the Golden Dawn assigned each Major Arcana card an astrological association and a Hebrew letter. Arthur Edward Waite, a Golden Dawn member and esoteric scholar and writer, switched the places of the Justice and Strength cards in the tarot deck he authored to allow their symbolism to fall more in line with the order of the signs of the zodiac. The deck was illustrated by Pamela Colman Smith and published by the Rider publishing company in 1910. The Smith-Waite deck is the most well-known tarot deck today. The Golden Dawn associations with Waite's order adjustment are the conventions followed in this book and the card order followed in both *Elemental Power Tarot* and *Tarot of Tales*, which are used to illustrate this book. In the Major Arcana chapter, you will see these cards presented in this order.

To assist with the use of the Major Arcana cards in ritual and to allow a deeper integration of their wisdom, crystal and apothecary associations are also provided. Some are traditional and some are more contemporary pairings. For the meanings of these associations, see pages 51–93.

Major Arcana Card	Astrological Association	Hebrew Letter
0 The Fool	Uranus	Aleph א
I The Magician	Mercury	Beth ב
II The High Priestess	Moon	Gimel ג
III The Empress	Venus	Daleth ד
IV The Emperor	Aries	He ה
V The Hierophant	Taurus	Vav (Waw) ו
VI The Lovers	Gemini	Zayin ז
VII The Chariot	Cancer	Heth ח
VIII Strength	Leo	Teth ט
IX The Hermit	Virgo	Yod י
X The Wheel of Fortune	Jupiter	Kaph כ
XI Justice	Libra	Lamed ל
XII The Hanged Man	Neptune	Mem מ
XIII Death	Scorpio	Nun נ
XIV Temperance	Sagittarius	Samekh ס
XV The Devil	Capricorn	Ayin ע
XVI The Tower	Mars	Pe פ
XVII The Star	Aquarius	Tsade צ
XVIII The Moon	Pisces	Qoph ק
XIX The Sun	Sun	Resh ר
XX Judgment	Pluto	Shin ש
XXI The World	Saturn	Tav (Taw) ת

Crystal	Apothecary Association	Affirmation
Peacock Ore	Bergamot	I immerse myself in the joy of here and now.
Labradorite	Cinnamon	I conjure my life through my words and actions every day.
Moonstone	Pomegranate, Jasmine	I commune easily with the spiritual and the earthly.
Aventurine	Rose	I give love freely and the world blooms.
Malachite	Cedar	I lead with vision, grace, and compassion.
Quartz Crystal	Frankincense	I honor the traditions of the past and make them my own to pass on.
Rhodonite	Vanilla	I embrace my weaknesses and offer my strengths.
Magnetite	Eucalyptus	I allow myself to be carried forward.
Carnelian	Ginger	I shine my light for the world to see.
Sodalite	Licorice	I study in solitude for the benefit of all.
Peridot	Nutmeg	I am exactly where and when I am supposed to be.
Tiger Eye	Olive	I treat myself and others fairly.
Lepidolite	Mushrooms	I turn my gaze in an unfamiliar direction to gain a new perspective.
Black Tourmaline	Myrrh	I release all that is not mine.
Scolecite	Sweet Violet	I spend my energy on my own terms.
Optical Calcite	Salt	I cut away the bindings of fear and doubt.
Rainbow Obsidian	Lavender	I trust the Universe to tear down what needs to be cleared.
Kunzite	Honey	I take my place in the eternal lineage of hope.
Iolite	Mint	I am stronger than my fears.
Citrine	Lemon	I open my eyes and my heart to the light of truth.
Fluorite	Clove	I determine my priorities and needs.
Amethyst	Angelica	I celebrate who I am and who I am becoming.

Exercise

Write down all of the Major Arcana cards (name and number) in a column on the left-hand side of a page in your tarot journal (see page 20). On the right-hand side, write down the names of people or characters that project the qualities of that card. These can be people you know personally, famous people, or characters from books, television, and movies. Keep going until you get three names for each card. This may take a while—you can come back to it over days or weeks and continue to update as you grow more familiar with the deck.

Card number	Meaning
Ace	Pure power
Two	Initial wisdom
Three	Collaboration
Four	Stability
Five	Chaos
Six	Achievement
Seven	Overcoming doubt
Eight	Longevity
Nine	Matured wisdom
Ten	Exaltation

Minor Arcana

The 56 cards of the Minor Arcana are divided into four suits, each containing ten numbered cards and four court cards. These cards dig into the details of daily life as we experience them and offer guidance on how to interact with and navigate through them.

Fortunately, you do not need to memorize 56 separate meanings to begin to understand these cards. Knowing the associations of the suits, numbers, and court roles gives you a big head start in gaining tarot fluency.

Each suit of the Minor Arcana corresponds to one of the four classical elements of Air (Swords), Fire (Wands), Water (Cups), and

Earth (Coins). The fifth element, Spirit, is associated with the Major Arcana. The numbered cards, Ace–10, explore the ways these elements show up in our lives and how they can influence our perspective. Each number represents a different aspect of the suit (see above). For example, threes speak to collaboration, so the Three of Cups is about emotional collaboration. Knowing these seeds of meaning can help you gain fluency and see relationships between cards in a spread more quickly.

The four court cards of each suit each have an elemental correspondence of their own: Page/Earth, Knight/Fire, Queen/Water, and King/Air. These cards show us how the elements can combine to bring out subtle (and sometimes not so subtle) aspects of their influence. Similar to the numbered cards, knowing the elemental nature of the court figure and the elemental nature of the suit gives you a quick shorthand for the energy of each card (see below). For example, Knights correspond to Fire, the element of action, creativity, and passion. The Knight of Cups represents the expression of that passion through the Water, the element of emotion, while the Knight of Swords expresses that same drive through Air, the element of intellect and communication.

To help you work with the elemental energies of the Minor Arcana, crystal and apothecary associations are provided for each suit on pages 95, 111, 127, and 143.

Exercise

Remove the Major Arcana cards from your deck. Pull Minor cards for a spread, then interpret that reading using only the charts opposite and below. Write down your thoughts, feelings, and hunches. Then check the dictionary of cards in this book (see pages 48–157) to see how your interpretation compares.

Doing this exercise regularly will help you gain confidence in your readings and give you insight into your own patterns and perspectives on the cards.

	Pages/Earth	Knights/Fire	Queens/Water	Kings/Air
Swords/ Air	PAGE OF SWORDS Earth of Air, The Novice of Communication	KNIGHT OF SWORDS Fire of Air, The Champion of Communication	QUEEN OF SWORDS Water of Air, The Nurturer of Communication	KING OF SWORDS Air of Air, The Strategist of Communication
Wands/ Fire	PAGE OF WANDS Earth of Fire, The Novice of Creation	KNIGHT OF WANDS Fire of Fire, The Champion of Creation	QUEEN OF WANDS Water of Fire, The Nurturer of Creation	KING OF WANDS Air of Fire, The Strategist of Creation
Cups/ Water	PAGE OF CUPS Earth of Water, The Novice of Emotion	KNIGHT OF CUPS Fire of Water, The Champion of Emotion	QUEEN OF CUPS Water of Water, The Nurturer of Emotion	KING OF CUPS Air of Water, The Strategist of Emotion
Coins/ Earth	PAGE OF COINS Earth of Earth, The Novice of Formation	KNIGHT OF COINS Fire of Earth, The Champion of Formation	QUEEN OF COINS Water of Earth, The Nurturer of Formation	KING OF COINS Air of Earth, The Strategist of Formation

III THE EMPRESS

TEN OF COINS

FIVE OF COINS

How the Parts of the Deck Fit Together

In practice, the numbered cards, court cards, and Major Arcana cards all work in concert to bring you the guidance you need. Our lives are a constant evolving mixture of the exalted and the mundane and each informs the other. Your readings will reflect that.

Some cards are natural "friends"; they have complementary energies that work well together. Others are in direct conflict. These spaces between the cards are just as important as the cards themselves. They are a part of the language of the deck.

For example, The Empress (see page 56) conveys a message of loving abundance, and the Ten of Coins (see page 153) presents an ideal of an abundant community. These two cards both indicate a sense of plenty and of mutual care and appreciation. They are in harmony.

The Five of Coins (see page 148) speaks to a fear of lack of resources. This energy is in conflict with that of The Empress (see page 56) and the Ten of Coins (see page 153). If the Five of Coins appears with either of these cards, a disconnect between perception and reality, or a misinterpretation of the situation in question, is possible.

Choosing Your Tarot Deck

If you're just starting out, I suggest you stick to using the same deck for a year. Build a relationship. Get to know your deck's quirks and eccentricities. Once you feel confident with one deck, your path to confidence with any other gets shorter and shorter.

The most important quality to look for in a tarot deck is magnetism—it has to draw you in. The reason it draws you in doesn't matter. You might have researched the artist/s who made it and appreciate their take on the cards, or maybe you just like cats and there are cats on the cards. Follow your impulse. There's something to it.

The other most important quality is tone. You're going to spend a lot of time with your tarot deck and be very vulnerable in your communication with it. If you are sensitive to severe language or imagery, you will have a better experience with a deck that has a more gentle and encouraging approach than you would with a deck that leans darker. Look at as many images as you can, see if you can find readers who have worked with the deck and shared their experience online, or go the old-fashioned route and walk into your local metaphysical shop and ask the witch behind the counter.

Strength

The World

The High Priestess

Caring For Your Deck

When you get your new deck home, make a ritual out of opening the package. Wash your hands, light some incense, put on music that makes you feel mystical. Open the package and take out the cards and the book if your deck comes with one. Feel the cardstock, examine the back of the cards. Then, go through the deck card by card, spending some time taking in each image. Once you have gone through all the cards, mix the cards up. I like to spread them all out face down and swirl them around. Then gather them back into a neat stack and shuffle them. A lot. Any way you shuffle is great.

After the cards are thoroughly shuffled, welcome your new confidante with this ritual using each of the five classical elements.

Water: Place a small dish of water beside the deck. The water will absorb any unneeded emotional energy.

Earth: Place a selenite or quartz crystal on top of your deck. Selenite is the universal cleanser of the mineral world. It helps to keep your deck from acquiring an energetic buildup while Quartz Crystal keeps your cards connected to Divine light.

Fire: Light incense. Frankincense is wonderful, but whatever you like will work.

Air: Using your hand or a feather, waft the incense smoke over the deck.

Spirit: Hold your deck with both hands, then close your eyes and visualize a beam of bright shimmering light reaching down from the universe into the top of your head and through your body and hands, into the cards.

When you are not using your cards, keep them in a safe place out of direct sun. If your deck comes in a sturdy box, you can continue to use that. If not, designate a small box or pouch to store your deck.

I like to keep a piece of selenite with my cards at all times. Selenite is a self-cleansing crystal that keeps your cards energetically fresh so you have a clean slate for each reading. Selenite is widely available at metaphysical shops and is fairly inexpensive.

Keeping a Tarot Journal

Keeping a tarot journal is one of the best ways to grow your relationship with your deck. Find a notebook and a pen or pencil that you enjoy writing with and use both only for this purpose. Every time you do a reading, notate the spread (see pages 34–47) along with your interpretations and any other thoughts, questions, impressions, or feelings it brings up.

Even if you are completely new to tarot and looking up every card in this book, writing down what you find in your own words helps you to develop your own style of the language of the cards and to retain the information so you can get "off book" more quickly. As you progress, you'll have a record of cards that make frequent appearances for you, how your impressions of certain cards shift in the context of other cards and questions, and your deepening understanding of yourself and your world.

Frequently Asked Questions

Don't I need to be gifted my first tarot deck?

Nope! This is a common bit of folk wisdom that gets passed around a lot and there is some benefit to it. Before the internet, the best way to ensure access to guidance around tarot reading for beginners was for all newbies to be invited by someone who already knew what they were doing. Personally, it feels a bit "gate-keepy" for me. I advocate for an open gate. Buy your own first deck. We are here waiting to help you.

What if someone else (maybe even someone I don't like) touches my cards?

Don't panic. Your cards are not tainted. Cleanse your cards using smoke, a bell (see page 30), or by placing a piece of selenite on top of the deck. In a pinch, wait until that person walks away, hold your cards in front of your face, take a deep intentional breath, and blow that touch right off of your deck.

XVI THE TOWER

I'm scared of getting bad news

This is not technically a question, but it is important to address. I am going to tell you something that will change your tarot life—there is no such thing as bad news. The cards want to help. Any information they give is actionable. So, if you see something in the cards that freaks you out, consider why and what you can do with that information. For example, if you are really into someone romantically and you ask about the situation and draw The Tower, even if that is an indication that this is NOT a good relationship for you (it isn't always, see The Tower on page 82), the cards are sparing you the heartbreak of pursuing something that's not in your best interest. Phew! What great, if not exactly pleasant, information to have.

What if I don't get the answer I want?

Wanting a specific answer is the easiest way to confuse yourself at best and trick yourself at worst. When we want a specific answer, usually that answer is yes. The cards do not like yes/no questions. If you rephrase that yes/no question as an open-ended question, then you will always get the answer you want, because the answer you want is the information you need to navigate your situation. "Is this person/job/place right for me?" becomes "How can I best move forward in this situation?" or "What do I need to know to choose the best path for me in this situation?" Don't you want those answers no matter what they are? Of course you do. That's why you're here.

When can I start reading for other people?

Whenever you want! However, you should be prepared to take care of that person emotionally, spiritually, and intellectually. People come to tarot readings open and vulnerable. They are placing their trust in you to offer guidance, often to help them with some aspect of their life they are confused by or having trouble with. Keeping your energy separate from someone else's while making them feel supported is called "holding space" and it is a skill you can learn and practice. We'll talk about how to do that in the next chapter (see page 33).

Trading readings with a friend who is also learning, or as part of a tarot meet up group, is a great way to get some experience in reading for others. Keep it light, keep it simple, and always offer a way forward, never a dead end.

How do I know who to trust?

Ah, the question as old as time! When you are seeking out guidance on reading tarot (or anything else really), consult a wide variety of sources and pay attention to how you feel in response to each. A good mentor for you is someone whose teachings make you feel both hopeful and challenged. Tarot is not all puppy dogs and rainbows. That doesn't mean it has to be painful or depressing. You're here because you feel called to look into yourself more deeply. Trust those who inspire you to keep following that star.

XVII THE STAR

CHAPTER 2

Reading the Map

To get the most out of your readings, you need to
understand how the individual meanings of the cards
come together to tell a story and plot a path forward.
This section contains step-by-step instructions on how
to do a tarot reading, including how to prepare, what to
look for, and how to read for others. You'll also learn
how tarot works as a language and what it can
and cannot do for you.

Finding Meaning

The language of tarot uses 78 cards to express all of the wisdom, guidance, and insight the universe has to offer. Each card relies not only on its own meaning, but also on its history, proximity, and relationship to other cards, and its personal resonance with the person doing the reading. While the core meanings of the cards evolve slowly over time like the words in any language, their significance in a particular reading takes on a rainbow of nuance depending on the context of the reading and the relationship between the reader and the querent.

Think of all the different things you can mean when you use phrases like "I'm sorry" or "stop it." They might be a sincere statement, a question, an exclamation of anger, delight, or surprise. Tarot functions similarly.

Gaining Fluency

As you become fluent in the language of tarot, you will develop your own style of speaking and reading. Gaining fluency takes time, dedication, patience, and practice. You wouldn't expect yourself to memorize the dictionary overnight and you wouldn't forbid yourself from speaking until you knew every word by heart. Tarot is no different.

We gain fluency in a language by challenging ourselves to communicate in that language, first in simple terms and broad strokes and then with more detail as we progress. Again, you do not need to memorize 78 separate card meanings to understand the basics of tarot. But it does help considerably to memorize the following 19 things in this order:

1 The elements of the suits and their meanings (five things). With only this information, you can see whether you are invited to approach your situation emotionally (Cups/Water),

KNIGHT OF CUPS

THE HANGED MAN

THE MOON

OF COINS

FIVE OF SWORDS

intellectually (Swords/Air), intuitively or creatively (Wands/Fire), materially (Coins/Earth), or spiritually (Major Arcana).

2 The meanings of the numbers (ten things)—see the chart on page 16. You can get the essence of each of the forty numbered cards by memorizing the meanings of the four suit elements and the ten numbered cards. For example, Three of Cups = Collaboration (Three) in the realm of emotion (Cups/Water).

3 The elemental associations of the court card roles and how they are personified (four things)—see the chart on page 17. Each of the sixteen court cards is a combination of two elemental energies, that of the suit and that of the role. By now, you already know the elements like the back of your hand. Memorizing the meanings of the four court card roles gives you the key to understanding all sixteen court cards across the deck.

Since the Major Arcana cards are based on archetypes most of us are at least a bit familiar with, you are now ready to begin to read "off book." Read daily, start with small spreads (see pages 36–39), and write down your thoughts, feelings, and impressions before consulting the dictionary of the cards in this book on pages 48–157. You'll be speaking tarot like a pro faster than you think.

Relationship Building

Develop a relationship with your deck. Do readings daily or at least a few times a week. Pulling one card is great. Keep your questions open-ended and as general as possible. Think of your readings as an ongoing conversation with a dear friend. You wouldn't call up a friend and demand an immediate answer to a yes or no question, would you? Of course not. It would be rude and you would be unlikely to get the wisdom you really needed. The same is true of your tarot deck. A quick temperature check on a situation is fine once in a while. Just try not to make it a habit.

What Tarot is Not

While tarot is an incredible tool for self-discovery, personal development, and navigating life, it has its limitations.

Tarot is not a medical professional. Questions regarding physical or mental health should always be used as a way of understanding your relationship to an issue, never as a form of diagnosis or treatment.

Tarot is not a view into the future. Tarot can help us focus our attention and understand our situation, but it cannot report a predetermined outcome. We all have free will within the circumstances of our lives at any given time.

Don't give away your power.

The future is yours to create.

Tarot is not a way to know what someone else is thinking. Doing a reading to see into another person's mindset is akin to spying. And that's if it's even accurate. Our own hopes and fears color our interpretation of the cards. This means tarot spying has the potential to mischaracterize someone's feelings and intentions and to seriously damage relationships. Stick to navigating your side of the relationship.

Tarot is not a marriage or relationship counselor. If you need some guidance on how to navigate an issue or what to focus on, the cards can help with that. If you have a serious issue or are questioning whether there is abuse happening in your relationship, that is a question for a professional or a trusted friend.

So what IS tarot good for?

Tarot thrives in an environment of open-minded exploration through open-ended questions. Think advice, not answers. Projection, not prediction. Tarot is a mirror and a storyteller. It can bring you peace and understanding, acceptance and wisdom.

PAGE OF CUPS

DEATH

OF COINS

OF SWORDS

FOUR OF WANDS

Drawing the Map

Now that you have some background on what to expect from your readings, let's look at how to do them in six easy steps.

1 **Clear the space. Pick up, sort out the clutter, sweep. Then cleanse the energy using smoke, spray, or a bell.**

Smoke cleanse

Sage and palo santo are the most common burnables for smoke cleanses, but there are many more for specific purposes. Ask the witch at your local metaphysical shop what they have and what they recommend for your purpose. Be mindful of where your burnables come from. Both white sage and palo santo are overharvested and are essential to Native American spiritual practices.

Cleansing spray

Due to the overharvesting of sage and palo santo, there are now a number of spiritual/energetic cleansing sprays available (including the one I make, MLH Energy Setting Spray). Cleansing sprays are more environmentally friendly and great for people who are sensitive to smoke. They are also wonderful for travel since most hotels frown on burning anything in their rooms.

Using a bell

Ringing a bell to clear energy (or chase away evil spirits) is a common practice in spiritual traditions around the world. Your bell can be rung by a clapper (which hangs down in the middle of the bell) or a mallet. Find one that has a tone you find pleasing and use it only for this purpose.

2 Clear your mind. If you have an existing meditation practice, do what you would normally do. If you don't, try this:

Soften your gaze. Slow your breath, breathing in for three counts and out for three counts. Let your eyes close if you like, or keep them open and fixed on one point. Feel your body being filled with bright shimmering light, starting in your heart and then radiating out through your torso, legs, arms, and head. The light fills your body and then it keeps growing, spilling out to fill the room. Stay here in this shimmering light for a few breath cycles, then when you are ready, blink your eyes open and come back into the moment.

3 Ask your question. Hold your tarot deck between the palms of your hands and think of your question. If you feel comfortable, ask it out loud, talking to your cards. They love company.

Ask open-ended questions. An open-ended question is one that cannot be answered with a simple "yes" or "no." The simplest way to ensure a question is open-ended is to start with the phrase "What guidance do I need around ____?" If you use this, your questions will always be open-ended. You can be general or specific. I like to start general and then zoom in, allowing the readings to inform each other as I go. For example, I might start with a three- or ten-card projection spread and ask, "What do the next six months look like for me?", then depending on what I see, I might move to "What guidance do I need around my work?" and then even "How can I best use my time in this project?"

Remember, this is like an intimate conversation with a trusted friend. Stay open-minded about what the cards have to say and trust that it is always in your best interest to receive the message.

4 **Shuffle the cards.** There is no right or wrong way to shuffle. Mix them up however you like. Shuffle to your heart's content (I really enjoy shuffling, so I usually do it for a while), at least three times. Then square the deck so all the cards are neatly in one stack, divide it into two piles (if you are reading for someone else, ask them to do this), and place the bottom pile on top of the other pile. Now you have a choice—you can divide the deck into three piles, choose one of those piles and draw your cards from the top down, or you can spread the cards all out and draw them one at a time. Try both and see what feels best for you.

5 **Lay out your spread (see pages 34–47), placing the cards face down as you pull them.**

6 **Once all cards are in place, flip them over and read your spread.** This is where all of your study, practice, and relationship building come in. Before you look anything up, check in with the four classical elements. Take notes on your elemental responses in your tarot journal.

Fire
What are you drawn to or repelled by? Is there a certain card, a color, an image, or a figure? Is there an area of the spread that seems especially important?

Water
How do you feel when you look at the cards? Do you have one strong feeling or is there a mix? Do you feel differently about certain cards?

Air
What do you think about the spread? What are the cards saying? Do you have questions? Is there another way to read the story in the cards?

Earth
How can you apply this information to your life? What can you do to integrate this information?

Now look up anything you want in this book. Does what you learned change any of your responses? Do you have more specific guidance to follow? Note your updates in your tarot journal.

Clarifying cards

Sometimes we get stuck on a card and can't quite pinpoint how it fits in a spread or what aspect of the card is at play. If this is the case, you can pull a clarifying card. If your cards are already spread out, just dip back in and grab another one. If you have three piles, continue to draw off of the pile you chose, or you can reshuffle while asking for clarification, then spread the cards out and draw one. Try to keep your clarifying cards to a minimum when you're starting out. Too much information can make your tarot vision blurry.

Challenges/Reversals

When a card is drawn upside down it is referred to as a challenge or reversal. Reversals are one way to read nuance in the meaning of the cards. In general, reversals can indicate a delay in the energy of the card, a more internal manifestation of the card's wisdom, or a difficulty in accepting or navigating a particular card's influence. Separate interpretations for reversed cards that offer more specific examples are given for the Major Arcana in this book. For the Minors, follow the general indications.

You can choose to read reversals or you can turn all your cards upright. You will not lose nuance. The information will come through in another way, whether it is a tension between cards in close proximity, a personal aversion or difficulty with the guidance of a card, or a gut feeling (another reason to check in with that Fire element!).

Decide whether you are going to read reversals before you lay the cards down and do what feels right for you.

Holding Space

When you read for others, it is important to hold space for the person you are reading for (the querent). Holding space for someone is the practice of creating a safe place for that person to be vulnerable. This means taking yourself out of that space to allow the reading to be about the querent and not about you. The easiest way to understand holding space is to imagine you are holding a bubble big enough for someone to sit inside. To hold the bubble in place and keep this person safe, you must remain outside of it.

Before you begin a reading, ask the querent to close their eyes and take three deep breaths with you, breathing in shimmering light and breathing out gray smoke. While you are breathing, visualize a bubble around the querent and a beam of light shining down into the top of your head, making your whole body glow. When you have finished your three breaths, open your eyes and proceed with the reading.

Holding space not only helps your querent feel calm and protected, it also keeps you from taking on their energy and ensures your energy stays out of the reading so you can provide more appropriate guidance. Your interpretation will always come through your personal perspective, but it will be more focused on the question and the person asking and what they need when you hold space.

Now, let's look at some spreads you can use to begin mapping out your life.

CHAPTER 3

Spreads

Spreads are the patterns used to lay out cards for readings. They bring structure to the messages from the cards and focus the guidance. In the language of tarot, the cards represent words and paragraphs. Spreads take these building blocks and combine them to make sentences and stories. When you choose a spread, you are asking the cards to converse with you in a specific format. You can ask the same question using different spreads to see a range of guidance.

Spreads get complex quickly as you add cards, so start small and build up to the bigger configurations as your understanding and fluency grow.

Single-card Spread

Yes, one card counts as a spread. Just as the word "no" can be a complete sentence, the guidance of one card can speak volumes. There are a few different ways to perform a single-card spread.

Card of the Day

This is a great way to gain familiarity with the deck and to focus the energy of your day. Since the reading is only for one day, keep your question open and simple. "What do I need to know today?" or "What energy am I invited to lead with today?" Or, if you are doing your reading at night, "What lesson can I take from today?"

General Questions

When asking general questions in a single-card spread, limit the scope by designating a timeframe. For example, if you want guidance around work, ask what you need to know this week/month/year. That way, the cards can be specific with you instead of giving you an overall life answer.

Specific Situations

For questions about particular situations, a single-card spread is an excellent way to get concise guidance without being overwhelmed. One card can provide direction to help you navigate a difficult dynamic with a co-worker, assess a possible job opportunity, or determine how to approach a family member to have a difficult conversation. If one card is not enough, pull a clarifying card (see page 33) before moving to a larger spread.

Three-card Spreads

Three-card spreads pack a lot of nuance into a limited amount of information. They are great for getting a concise read on a situation, for focusing your attention or energy, and for beginners to gain familiarity with the cards and practice reading them in combination. These two spreads are intended for general use. Use them to gain insight into an area of life, a period of time, or a specific situation. Decide in advance which format you are using.

Past, Present, Future

Exactly what it sounds like. This spread gives you a view into the linear development of your topic or question.

CARD 1: Shows influences and concerns that contributed to and informed where you are now.

CARD 2: Represents your current situation.

CARD 3: Offers guidance on how the situation will naturally develop from where you are now.

What if the future looks bleak or hard or just not what you want? The cards do not tell you your future, they give you information. If you don't like where things are headed, this is a great opportunity for you to reconsider your approach in the present or even to go back to look at where this came from to see if the past changes how you feel about the present.

If you are left confused about how to move forward, go back to the cards. Either in your heart or out loud, ask "how can I best move forward?" then pull a fourth card from the deck and place it to the right and above Card 3.

CARD 1   CARD 2   CARD 3

What's It All About?

Placing Card 1 in the center of your spread with the other two cards on either side gives a view into the intersecting energies, personalities, and desires contributing to a situation.

CARD 1: Represents the core nature of the situation, the energy that is either most present or most felt.

CARD 2: Shows how you have interpreted the situation or what you want from it.

CARD 3: Offers guidance on how to move forward.

What if Card 3 is a "bad" or "negative" card? No cards are bad cards. They all offer valuable information. For example, if you pull The Devil in this position, that is an indication that you need to find an obstacle (a habit, a way of thinking, a long-standing limiting belief) that is holding you back and work to release yourself from it before taking any other steps.

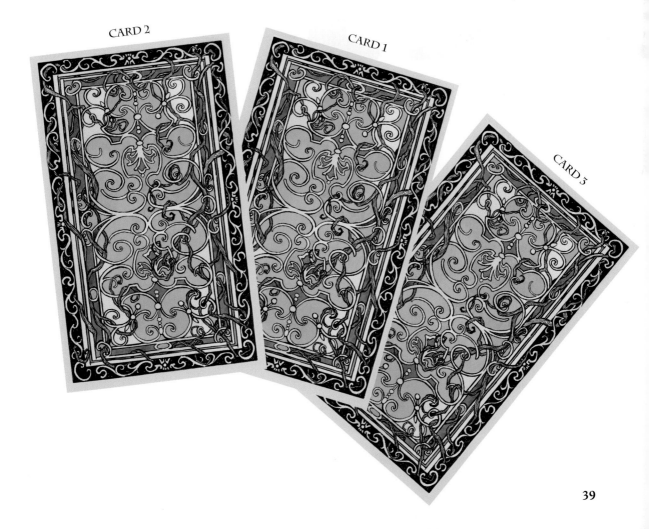

CARD 2   CARD 1   CARD 3

Once you've had some practice conversing with the cards, you can expand your discussions by working with larger spreads. Since every card in a spread affects the energy of every other card, the complexity of the message increases exponentially with each additional card. So don't get down on yourself if the larger spreads seem incomprehensible at first. Test the waters of the four- and five-card spreads and work your way up. With practice, reading ten cards and more will be smooth sailing for you.

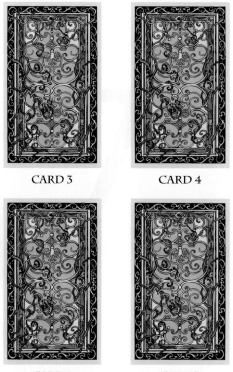

CARD 3   CARD 4

CARD 1   CARD 2

Four-card Spread: Finding Stability

A plan for getting grounded and clearing confusion in any situation, area of life, or time period.

Ask "How can I gain stability in _____?"

CARD 1: What you can do right now to feel more grounded.
CARD 2: The path that opens through this grounding.
CARD 3: A new way of seeing your situation.
CARD 4: How you grow through this process.

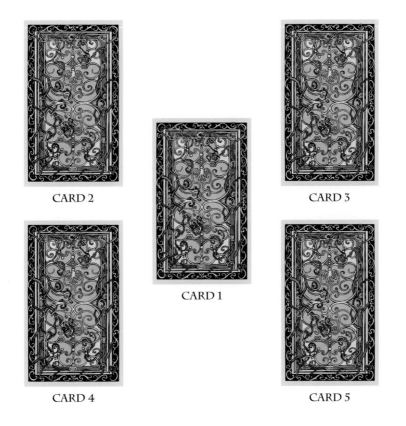

CARD 2

CARD 3

CARD 1

CARD 4

CARD 5

Five-card Spread: As Above So Below

A way of understanding how inner and outer
forces work together to facilitate growth.

Ask "How can I better understand _____?"

CARD 1: The nature of the situation.
CARD 2: What the situation is drawing your
attention to.
CARD 3: How you can change the situation.
CARD 4: What you can learn from this situation.
CARD 5: How you are changed by this situation.

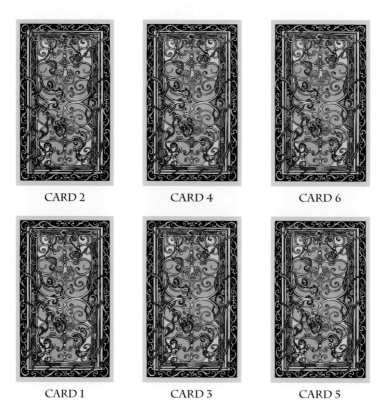

CARD 2   CARD 4   CARD 6

CARD 1   CARD 3   CARD 5

Six-card Spread: Love and Understanding

This spread can be read in two different ways depending on whether you are looking for guidance on how to find love or in need of insight into your current relationship. In both cases, the bottom row focuses on you and the top row focuses on the potential or current relationship.

Looking For Love

CARD 1: What you want from a relationship.
CARD 2: What you need from a relationship.
CARD 3: What you offer in relationships.
CARD 4: How your offer is received.
CARD 5: How to approach relationships.
CARD 6: What to look for in a partner.

In a Relationship

CARD 1: What you want from this relationship.
CARD 2: What you need from this relationship.
CARD 3: What you offer to your partner.
CARD 4: How your offer is received by your partner.
CARD 5: How to approach communication with your partner.
CARD 6: What to expect from your partner.

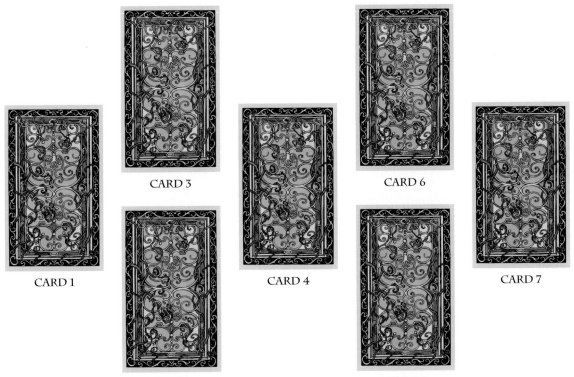

CARD 3

CARD 6

CARD 1

CARD 4

CARD 7

CARD 2

CARD 5

Seven-card Spread: Career Development

This spread can be used to gain insight into your overall career, a project, or a position. You can add a time element to this spread by asking "What does my career/project/job look like over the next month/year/5 years?"

CARD 1: Where you are now in your career.

CARD 2: Where you hope to be.

CARD 3: How to get there.

CARD 4: The next phase of your career.

CARD 5: The biggest challenge of the next phase.

CARD 6: How to overcome this challenge.

CARD 7: The energy that supports you through it all.

Ten-card Spread: The Path Ahead/ Levels of Consciousness

This is a modified Celtic Cross spread. The right-hand column has been moved up to create horizontal lines in the spread representing three levels of consciousness. This is the spread I use most in my personal readings because it offers both insight into what is going on under the surface in the subconscious (deep within) and overhead in the hyperconscious (loudest influences), and gives a projection through time.

This spread can be used for specific questions, areas of life, or periods of time.
Ask "What is my path in _____?"

CARD 1: Where you are now.
CARD 2: The energy swirling around you.
CARD 3: The biggest influence on you.
CARD 4: The inner force driving your decision making.
CARD 5: How you got to this point, a lesson learned in the past.
CARD 6: The next step in your journey.
CARD 7: Who you believe you are.
CARD 8: How others see you, what you can resolve.
CARD 9: Your hopes and fears.
CARD 10: The key to unlocking the wisdom you can gain through this process.

CARD 10

CARD 3

CARD 9

CARD 2

CARD 5

CARD 1

CARD 6

CARD 8

CARD 4

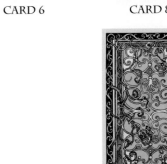

CARD 7

Twelve-card Spread: The Year Ahead

This is a great spread to do at the start of the calendar year, but you can start it any time of the year to get a view into the next twelve months. When you start in January, you have the benefit of seeing a theme for each season as delineated by the solstices and equinoxes in the rows.

Note all of the cards in your tarot journal, then write each at the top of the page for 12 pages. At the end of each month, go back and fill in the page with your reflections on how the card spoke to your experience of that month.

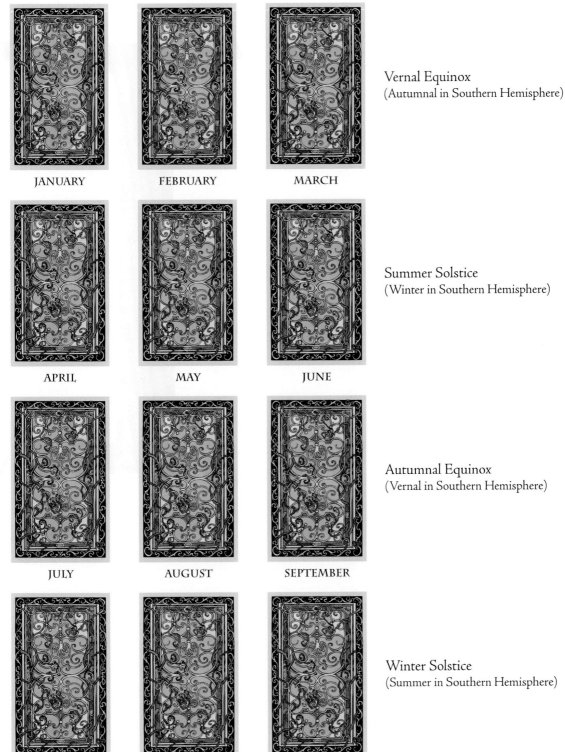

JANUARY

FEBRUARY

MARCH

Vernal Equinox
(Autumnal in Southern Hemisphere)

APRIL

MAY

JUNE

Summer Solstice
(Winter in Southern Hemisphere)

JULY

AUGUST

SEPTEMBER

Autumnal Equinox
(Vernal in Southern Hemisphere)

OCTOBER

NOVEMBER

DECEMBER

Winter Solstice
(Summer in Southern Hemisphere)

CHAPTER 4

Major Arcana

Some of the Major Arcana cards are named for a person
in a role—The Fool or The Magician, for example.
Others are named for entities, concepts, or virtues that
were commonly personified in the morality plays
of medieval Europe—Temperance, Death, The Sun,
and The Moon. In tarot, all of these cards can be
both characters to embody and wisdom to employ.
Think of each of them as something you can be
and something you can do.

0 The Fool

The Fool teaches us the joy of living in the present moment. When you are visited by The Fool in a reading, let go of regrets and nostalgia from the past, and fears and fantasies about the future. Now is what matters. Bring your awareness into your immediate surroundings. Take a deep breath. Give yourself over to the pleasures of where you are and what you have right here and now.

Practicing Presence

Being present does not come naturally for most people. It takes practice. Start simple. Set a timer for one minute, close your eyes, and focus your attention on your breath, noticing how it feels in your nostrils, your throat, your lungs. Feel the expansion of your diaphragm and its contraction as the air is pushed back out. One minute will probably feel like an eternity when you begin. Keep going. It will get easier and you may find yourself growing an interest in other forms of meditation.

Projection Spreads

In projection spreads, The Fool calls for a time out from the daily grind. Take it seriously. There could be information available that will alter the course of action you take, information you can only receive if you are free from distractions. Quiet your mind and your life enough to hear it and be open to any possibility.

Love and Relationships

If you are looking for love and The Fool comes up, the good news is, there is nothing for you to do right now. The bad news is, there is nothing for you to do right now. Keep living your life day by day and see who wanders into the scene. Also, consider going to a meditation class. Meditation is all about cultivating presence and sometimes the cards are very direct and pragmatic. You might meet a like-minded soul.

If you are in a relationship, you are likely asking about it because there is something about the dynamic that is bothering you. Leave it be. You don't need to talk it out, you don't need to do anything. Accept things as they are for now, enjoy today, and see what happens.

Career and Money

In money matters, The Fool can be a very good omen, implying a possibility of "pennies from heaven." Keep a little space open in your schedule to make room for surprise opportunities. If you are working, keep it status quo. If you're looking for work, something could fall into your lap if you are open to it.

Challenge/Reversal

The intense presence of The Fool can look and feel like a stall. Remember that, though it may look like it from the outside, cultivating presence is not doing nothing. It is an extremely valuable activity and skill. Watch for negative thoughts about yourself and invite them to float away gently down a forest stream.

0 THE FOOL

The Fool

Astrological Association

Uranus is the rebel of the astrological planetary family, but the rebelliousness is not without cause. Uranus breaks the rules to find a new, more enlightened way.

Hebrew Letter: א

The letter Aleph represents conception, the moment that unity becomes the promise of plurality. It corresponds to the path on the Tree of Life connecting Kether (crown) and Chokmah (wisdom).

Crystal

Peacock Ore. Brings the ethereal body into balance to support contentment.

Apothecary

Bergamot. Promotes joy and soothes stress.

Affirmation

I immerse myself in the joy of here and now.

I The Magician

The Magician teaches us that we hold the power to shift our reality by the force of our will, our own personal magick. When this card comes up in a reading, it is an indication that you have more freedom and more ability than you may think to change your situation. Step into your power. Accept that you can move mountains with your magick.

All Words are Magick Words

The Magician is associated with Mercury, planet of communication. How do you speak about your situation? Your place within it? Do you speak differently about it to yourself than you do to others? Words exist in the realm of Air. The Magician is the master of all of the elements, so be sure to check in with each. What is your emotional (Water) response? Where is your instinct (Fire) pulling you toward or pushing you away from? How can you change your relationship to your body and/or environment (Earth) to align with your desired path in his situation?

I THE MAGICIAN

The Magician

Projection Spreads

In projection spreads, The Magician indicates a time to create your own path rather than finding one to follow. Strike while the iron is hot. While this can be a long-term leveling up of powers, they will be most potent in the time period given in the spread.

Love and Relationships

When looking for love, The Magician can be a great gift or a great frustration. You hold the power to create the situation you desire (and/or the one that is best for you). Know what you want? Great! Go for it, see it, feel it, make it so. If you don't know what you want, The Magician can be an invitation to take a step back from actively searching for a partner. Instead, turn your attention to creating the love and companionship you seek in a relationship within yourself.

For those in a relationship, The Magician provides an opportunity to shift the dynamic of the relationship through sheer will. Check on your magick words and all of your elemental responses and make sure you're making the shift you want, not the one you fear.

Career and Money

If you've been wondering if you should break away from routine and strike out on your own, The Magician is a resounding yes. This is great support for creatives and entrepreneurs. If you're staying in your current position, you have the power to make it what you want. The Magician has the alchemical power to turn lead into gold.

Challenge/Reversal

The immense force of The Magician follows the will of the person wielding it. This means that it can be used to lift up or to weigh down, to encourage expansion or stifle growth. Take stock of where your energy is going. If you are not careful, you could end up working against your own best interests.

Astrological Association

Mercury, planet of communication, is named after the Roman god of travelers Mercury, also known as Hermes, the messenger god of Greek mythology.

Hebrew Letter: ב

The letter Beth represents duality, Human/Deity, mortal/immortal, life/death. It corresponds to the path on the Tree of Life connecting Kether (crown) and Binah (understanding).

Crystal

Labradorite. Activates and enhances one's inherent magickal powers.

Apothecary

Cinnamon. Accelerates the working of spells and rituals.

Affirmation

I conjure my life with my words and actions every day.

II The High Priestess

The High Priestess teaches us to identify and protect the sacred in our lives. Look first to your spiritual practices and beliefs to find any neglected rituals. Then broaden your view to include your home, your body. How do you define your temple? What boundaries can you strengthen to ensure you can care for your temple in a way that reflects your beliefs and values?

Moving Between Worlds

The work of the High Priestess involves traveling from the world of the mundane (daily life) to the world of the sacred and back again. This is done by honoring your deities, spirits, guides, and ancestors through ritual and reflection. These rituals can be complex or simple, traditional or modern, learned or created. What is important is that they are aligned with your personal beliefs and intentions and that you can reasonably fit them into your life. The High Priestess promises solace and restoration for those who work to maintain their temple. Look around your home. What do you see that feels most *you*? If there isn't anything, what is accessible to you that would? How is your spiritual self represented in your worldly space?

Projection Spreads

The High Priestess indicates you may need more time and space alone to hear your own voice, consult the Divine, and make your own decisions. Be prepared to say no to invites and social functions to tend to your own needs. This is a time for reflecting and elevating spiritually and personally.

Love and Relationships

Boundaries, boundaries, boundaries. If you are looking for love, The High Priestess can be a message to keep potential dates or partners at arm's length for now. Whether this is because you have some personal development to get through or because there aren't any suitable candidates in the mix, the guidance is the same—focus on yourself.

If you are in a relationship, make sure you are giving yourself what you need as an individual as well as a partner. If you are cohabitating, try to find space in your home that is just for you. Your attention to yourself will benefit your partner and family.

Career and Money

The High Priestess favors the transcendent and the mystical. This card does not promise or support big career growth. Don't be discouraged. There is something to be discovered through reflection and ritual that will help you move forward. If you have been under pressure to make a decision, give yourself a break. An answer will come when it is time.

Challenge/Reversal

There is a fine line between alone and lonely. Take steps to avoid crossing it. Your boundaries may be so strong that they are isolating you. Be more flexible with your rules and try to be vulnerable with yourself and others. Let go of any fear keeping you from contemplating your life and purpose.

II THE HIGH PRIESTESS

The High Priestess

Astrological Association

The Moon, our closest neighbor, has great influence on our emotions. The Moon illuminates our path in the darkness, watching over us.

Hebrew Letter: ג

The letter Gimel represents fruition, the spiritual made material. It corresponds to the path on the Tree of Life connecting Kether (crown) and Tiphareth (beauty).

Crystal

Moonstone. Soothes emotion and opens up intuition.

Apothecary

Pomegranate. Facilitates travel between worlds. Jasmine. Promotes lunar wisdom and prophetic dreams.

Affirmation

I commune easily with the spiritual and the earthly.

III The Empress

The Empress teaches us that generosity and love are the keys to growing true abundance. When The Empress appears, there is a great opportunity for organic growth with you at the center. Open your heart and let your love flow freely with no fear of depletion. The more you give, the more you will receive. Let the nourishment of your heart feed the garden of your life.

Expect Acceptance

When you walk into a room, do you feel like you have to prove yourself? Do you anticipate being scrutinized? What would it feel like to default to believing you will be accepted, embraced even? What do you have to lose by trying? We often think of expecting acceptance as a type of arrogance, but it's really a kind world view, one in which we are all awesome until proven otherwise and treat each other accordingly.

III THE EMPRESS

The Empress

Projection Spreads

Seeing The Empress in your future is a wonderful gift. Make room for socializing and for activities or hobbies that you love. The Empress naturally attracts prosperity, but does not seek it out or force it. Be open and optimistic. If you have a passion project or goal, throw all of your heart into it without expectation of a specific outcome. Let it grow wild and free.

Love and Relationships

Whether you are in love or looking for love, The Empress indicates that your heart's true source of fulfillment is you. Love yourself unconditionally and you will attract the love you desire. This card is also an indication that your inner and outer beauty is seen by others. You are invited to move through the dating pool or within your relationship as the beautiful, regal, splendorous creature that you are.

Career and Money

Whatever you pour your heart into will grow and flourish. You may not see your gain in the form of money. Abundance comes in many forms. You could see an increase in support for your ideas at work, a generous benefits package, an offer of supplies or space to pursue a project, opportunities to get your work out into the world. Accept any and all contributions with grace and gratitude. Any of them could end up being the key to future financial success.

Challenge/Reversal

Relying on organic growth requires a large amount of trust. This trust can be hard to come by if you are in a tough spot financially or emotionally. Additionally, if you choose to give your love and attention to something that does not serve you (an unhealthy relationship for example), you could end up with an abundance of heartache.

Astrological Association

Venus is the planet of love and beauty. It is the brightest point of light we see in the night sky, outshone only by the Sun and the Moon.

Hebrew Letter: ד

The letter Daleth represents realization, care made apparent. It corresponds to the path on the Tree of Life connecting Chokmah (wisdom) and Binah (understanding).

Crystal

Aventurine. Increases love and its fruits.

Apothecary

Rose. Opens, soothes, and expands the heart.

Affirmation

I give love freely and the world blooms.

IV The Emperor

The Emperor teaches us that leadership is an art, not a science. We all express leadership in our own personal way, drawing on our individual strengths and gifts. It is not enough to demand or provoke action. We must find how to best inspire others to join us in pursuing and actualizing our vision. The highest incarnation of Emperor energy is a cunning commander whose primary objective is the wellbeing of all.

I'm Not Bossy, I'm the Boss

Successful leadership is more about how direction is received than how it is given. When getting ready to be the boss in any situation, it is important to know how those you are leading are best motivated. This includes yourself. If you know you are motivated by praise, do not berate yourself when you stumble.

Projection Spreads

In a projection spread, The Emperor signals a time when you are called to stand up and take charge. You cannot watch from the sidelines, waiting for something to happen. You are the something. You make it happen. How you take charge is up to you. You could use this time to make a big, public pronouncement or you might shift your mindset, quietly directing how you spend your time and energy. No matter what you do, people will follow your lead.

Love and Relationships

When looking for love, The Emperor strongly suggests that you take a more active role in dating. Be the one to call, to make dates, set the pace. If the thought of this makes you want to hide under a blanket, consider doing one active thing in your search for love. Accept an invitation to socialize with friends, make eye contact with a stranger, update your profile pic. Push the boundary of your comfort level, wherever that is for you.

If you are in a relationship, it is your responsibility to steer the boat. No matter what caused the stormy seas you're sailing, you need to get control of the vessel and get it safely back to shore. In non-nautical terms: It doesn't matter who started the fight. End it, with the love and compassion you would want to receive. Even if there is no conflict and no issues, pick a direction and start steering your relationship toward it.

Career and Money

If you have always thought about starting your own business, but never knew if the time was right, now it is. People will see your vision. You can get ahead in your career, but you have to take action. The Emperor gets what The Emperor makes happen.

Challenge/Reversal

Leadership can easily slip into domination and tyranny. Take care to use it generously, not selfishly. Don't pull the ladder up when you get to the next level. Reach down and help the next person climb up.

IV THE EMPEROR

The Emperor

Astrological Association

Aries, the ram, is the first sign of the zodiac, bravely blazing a trail for all others.

Hebrew Letter: ה

The letter He represents form, the completion of ideation. It corresponds to the path on the Tree of Life connecting Chokmah (wisdom) and Tiphareth (beauty).

Crystal

Malachite. Promotes heart-centered leadership, luck, and prosperity.

Apothecary

Cedar. Offers strength, protection, and power of the ancients.

Affirmation

I lead with vision, grace, and compassion.

V The Hierophant

The Hierophant, the great teacher of the tarot, invites us to be closer to the Divine through a spiritual lineage of learning. That lineage could be passed down through books, formal study, or one-on-one mentorship. If you do not see yourself in any tradition right now, be open to accepting a teacher. This is an initiation. You are ready to receive a higher level of wisdom than you ever have before.

Student Teacher

You will always know more than someone and less than someone about any topic you study. In the pursuit of spiritual and magickal knowledge it is very important to remember this. No matter how much you study and learn and practice, there is always more mystery in the Universe. Think of it like being a permanent student teacher. You know enough to teach others, but still have more to learn.

Context informs meaning. Consider whether there are aspects of your tradition that need updating to maintain relevance today. For example, tarot imagery and language

V THE HIEROPHANT

The Hierophant

is traditionally very Eurocentric and strictly gendered, owing to its origins in medieval Europe, but today many of us have moved to more inclusive language and imagery in accordance with contemporary culture.

Projection Spreads

When The Hierophant appears on your path, things are about to get serious. There is a focus on prioritizing the things in your life that are most in alignment with your spirituality. This can be a wonderful time of self-love and acceptance that brings deeper meaning to every part of your life. It can also be an opportunity for re-learning what spiritual beliefs and practices can look like and which ones resonate most with you.

Love and Relationships

If you are looking for love, The Hierophant asks you to first find love in yourself and in the Divine, then use that love to set a standard for your potential partners. Casual dating is not supported by this card, but the pursuit of deep, meaningful, spiritual connection is.

If you are in a relationship, try viewing it through a spiritual lens. What role do each of you play in the other's personal evolution? What are you learning in your relationship? What are you teaching? What values do you hold as a couple? If you cohabitate, how are those values reflected in your home and your daily rituals? The intellectual nature of The Hierophant can make the discussion of emotional issues more productive and less volatile.

Career and Money

The Hierophant brings a critical eye to money matters. Is money the most important thing to be asking about right now? Are you in danger of compromising your ethics in the pursuit of career advancement? Focus on long-term goals and personal investments that rise to your level.

Challenge/Reversal

You may find you are committed to a spiritual tradition or teacher that you no longer believe in, or a revered teacher may behave in a way that is shocking or repellent to you. It is healthy to question authority and institutions. Take time to rediscover what you believe and explore different teachings.

Astrological Association

Taurus, the bull, is the oldest constellation in the zodiac, dating back to use as a marker of the Spring Equinox (in the Northern Hemisphere) before the Bronze Age.

Hebrew Letter: ו

The letter Vav (Waw) represents connection, contact established and accepted. It corresponds to the path on the Tree of Life connecting Chokmah (wisdom) and Chesed (mercy).

Crystal

Quartz Crystal. Amplifies the power of all other crystals, opens the crown to receive spiritual wisdom.

Apothecary

Frankincense. Facilitates Divine connection.

Affirmation

I honor the traditions of the past and make them my own to pass on.

VI The Lovers

The Lovers teaches us that true lasting partnership is built on complementary differences. Whether romantic, platonic, creative, or business, partnership is much more about practical compatibility than it is about attraction. Attraction is the initial spark. Mutually beneficial skill sets are the glue that holds a partnership together.

Embracing Weakness

Assessing partnership potential requires us to look closely at what we lack. When you know and embrace both your strengths and your weaknesses, you are better equipped to attract and choose a suitable partner of any type. Your weaknesses are not flaws and they are not shameful. They exist to give you the space and energy for your strengths to thrive. In that sense, you can be thankful for them.

We all grow up with messages around what we should and should not be good at based on who we are, our gender, sexuality, age, culture, ethnicity. These messages can create a lot of problems if we measure our gifts with their ruler. Let go of any "shoulds" and be appreciative of your specific skill set. It gives you a map to find a great partner.

Projection Spreads

When The Lovers comes up in a spread that is not specifically about love or business, it can indicate someone coming into your life that is a great match for you in some way. Keep an eye out for people who are impressed by what you're good at. You may not partner up immediately, but they could be important to you in the future.

Love and Relationships

This is one of the most welcome cards you can get in a love spread. The trick is, you've got to be prepared to be practical. Despite its name, The Lovers does not promise a torrid affair (that's more of a Two of Cups + Knight of Wands situation). What it does promise is the potential for a lasting, stable, and fulfilling relationship. If you're not ready for that quite yet, see if you can use this energy to identify who would be good for you and keep tabs on that person until you are.

If you are in a relationship, this is an excellent indicator of a deepening of the relationship and of a growth in appreciation each of you has for the other.

Career and Money

The Lovers is an especially useful energy for entrepreneurs seeking business partnerships, but it is also great for anyone in need of an ally at work. In money matters, it could indicate the need for a partner to reach your goal.

Challenge/Reversal

For a partnership to be successful, both parties must give the other the space to be an individual. Take care not to lose yourself. The value you add to the equation lies in your unique experience and perspective. If you feel pressured to change who you are, this is not the right partnership for you.

VI THE LOVERS

The Lovers

Astrological Association

Gemini is the sign of the twins, the constellation formed around the twin stars Castor and Pollux from Greek mythology and earlier, the Great Twins of Babylonian astronomy.

Hebrew Letter: ז

The letter Zayin represents power, dynamic potential. It corresponds to the path on the Tree of Life connecting Binah (understanding) and Tiphareth (beauty).

Crystal

Rhodonite. Inspires compassion and love for others.

Apothecary

Vanilla. Strengthens and calms relationships.

Affirmation

I embrace my weaknesses and offer my strengths.

VII The Chariot

The Chariot teaches us to accept help when we need it. This card is named for the vehicle, not the driver. We all need different types of assistance at different times, different vehicles that can get us where we need to go. And The Chariot is not just any vehicle, it is a special purpose-built vehicle just for you that arrives right when you need it. All you have to do is step in.

Let Go of the Reins

Don't let your chariot pass you by because you don't recognize the driver. The help you need may come from an unlikely place or person. When you see The Chariot in a reading, that is your signal to perk up your ears and assess your situation. Try to identify multiple areas you could use help in and what that help could look like—not where it could come from. In order to accept help, you have to let go of some control. Help the Universe help you by simply being ready to receive.

VII THE CHARIOT

The Chariot

Projection Spreads

The Chariot can be a speed bump or a fast lane depending on how you approach it. Whatever your plans are, be ready to change them. It will be for the better. You may end up on a very different route but you will get to your destination a little faster and much better equipped.

Love and Relationships

While The Chariot is a somewhat practical card, it is associated with Cancer, bringing a sense of nurturing and care into the mix. If you are looking for love, look for someone who makes you feel cared for, like you can sit back and be a passenger sometimes.

If you are in a relationship, let your partner take care of you. You can even ask for it. If you do, try to be specific about the request, but open about the delivery. For example, if you would like your partner to be responsible for dinner, leave it to them whether they want to cook, get take out, or take you out on a date.

Career and Money

In a money reading, The Chariot is a bit of a mystery prize box. You don't know what's in it, but it's going to be to your benefit. A need for money could be helped by getting a raise, landing a side gig, selling property, or receiving a gift. A career boost could come in the form of a promotion, a new connection, an unforeseen project, or some other opportunity. Whatever it is, it will be tailor-made just for your situation.

Challenge/Reversal

We all need a lift sometimes, but it can be hard to admit it. If you have a tendency to be a little too self-sufficient, The Chariot can be a difficult energy to work with. If this is the case, let this card be more of a personal development signal than a practical one. You could have trouble recognizing help when it comes and grow frustrated forging ahead on your own.

Astrological Association

Cancer is the natural nurturer of the zodiac, able to tap into the emotional needs of others to soothe and protect.

Hebrew Letter: ח

The letter Heth represents forces united in cause. It corresponds to the path on the Tree of Life connecting Binah (understanding) and Geburah (severity).

Crystal

Magnetite. Naturally magnetic, both physically and energetically.

Apothecary

Eucalyptus. Eases exhaustion and brings mental clarity.

Affirmation

I allow myself to be carried forward.

VIII Strength

Strength teaches us that our greatest power is seen and felt even when we are still. Perhaps most when we are still. In a society that teaches us we must always be doing more, making more, consuming more, it takes guts to do less, to be gentle. True strength is doing what you know is best for you and others even when it goes against norms and expectations.

Shine Like the Sun

The Strength card urges us to uncover our own personal type of power and beam it out into the world. We all bring an energy into any room we enter. You can choose what that energy will be, the presence you have. You are strong. Your strength is unique to you. Embrace it and broadcast it just by existing in a certain time and space. We see and feel the presence of the sun before it peeks up over the horizon. Let your light announce your arrival.

Projection Spreads

When and where Strength shows up on your path, you can expect to have great influence over events in your life if you do not fight your circumstances. Depending on what other cards are present, this could be a time when you need to step into a position of power, officially or unofficially, or you may be called to stand your ground. Lead with kindness and trust that your opinions will come through loud and clear with very little effort on your part.

Love and Relationships

Your powers of attraction get a boost from Strength in the best way. Show off your power, set the dynamic, be magnetic. Magnetism isn't about figuring out how to draw a specific person in, it's about tapping into your personal *je ne sais quoi* and projecting it out so you attract someone who appreciates your allure.

If you are looking for love, know that people feel your presence strongly in a room, so be particular about the rooms you choose to grace and who you give your attention to.

If you are in a relationship, take the initiative to stoke or reignite the flame.

Career and Money

With Strength on your side, you exude competence and inspire trust. If you need to ask for approval or permission for anything in your career, this energy is excellent support for that. Money and opportunities can flow to you, but you've got to put yourself out there to get them. Creatives and entrepreneurs get a boost of recognition and appreciation for their work.

Challenge/Reversal

Be careful not to mistake confidence for arrogance. Keeping yourself small to avoid seeming arrogant is just as damaging as crossing over confidence into actual arrogance. Either way you miss out on a time to let your true self shine.

VIII STRENGTH

Strength

Astrological Association

Leo is symbolized by the lion, a beast with unmistakable power, whether hunting or napping in the sun.

Hebrew Letter: ט

The letter Teth represents purity, the absence of doubt. It corresponds to the path on the Tree of Life connecting Geburah (severity) and Tiphareth (beauty).

Crystal

Carnelian. The warrior's stone, brings stamina and courage.

Apothecary

Ginger. The heat of ginger activates elemental Fire for increased vitality and creativity.

Affirmation

I shine my light for the world to see.

IX The Hermit

The Hermit teaches us the importance of purposeful solitude. In our modern vernacular, a hermit is a recluse, usually odd and often a bit scary. In the language of tarot, The Hermit is a figure of great wisdom who retreats in order to process and synthesize information and ideas that they bring back out to benefit the community.

Seeds of Invention

There is a "mad scientist" quality to The Hermit. Huddled alone in piles of books and papers, poring over research and data from experiments, searching for the one thing that connects it all. The Hermit invents something new that will light the way for others, even if its importance isn't recognized right away. Nikola Tesla was considered a mad scientist in his day and he invented the tesla coil—still used in wireless transmission technology today—in 1891.

IX THE HERMIT

The Hermit

Projection Spreads

The Hermit indicates you are going to be taking some time away and it's best if you can take the lead in planning for it. If you don't, the Universe may step in to "help" and it may not be the most convenient time for you.

Love and Relationships

In love readings, The Hermit does not mean you will spend your life alone. It does mean you have some stuff to work out on your own before you dive into anything serious. You already have all of the information gathered, you just need to spend some dedicated time putting the pieces together to find what they mean.

If you are in a relationship, take some time for yourself. Even a walk around the block alone will do wonders. We can't all run off to a misty mountaintop (though if you can, go for it!). Do what works for you and your life.

Career and Money

Though it may not seem like it, The Hermit is a great career card. You are invited to gather up all of your past skills, experiences, and accomplishments and sit with them for a bit, mix them up, find different ways they fit together and complement each other. You could discover a completely new career path, one that you are uniquely qualified for.

In money matters as well, there is a need to gather up what you know and spend time turning it over, looking at it from different angles, bringing in some more information to find a new way of bringing in money that grows out of how you've been operating.

Challenge/Reversal

The Hermit demands a lot of work from you. You may not be in a place where it is easy to make time and space for this work or you may just not feel like it. How and how much you engage with The Hermit is up to you. You may need to make a lot of tough choices to dive into this work, but the rewards can be life changing.

Astrological Association

Virgo is represented by the maiden, or virgin, which originally was not related to sexual experience, but to spiritual purity suitable for temple keeping.

Hebrew Letter: ׳

The letter Yod represents universality, the individual within the collective. It corresponds to the path on the Tree of Life connecting Chesed (mercy) and Tiphareth (beauty).

Crystal

Sodalite. Stimulates attention and diligence to stick to and complete tasks.

Apothecary

Licorice. Soothes the body and the mind.

Affirmation

I study in solitude for the benefit of all.

X The Wheel of Fortune

The Wheel of Fortune teaches us that Divine timing may not always meet our expectations, but it is always in service of our greatest good. This card is a celebration with a caveat. Things are working out in your favor, but you have to be patient and open in terms of how and when you see them come to fruition. Enjoy the energy you save by allowing and not pushing for results. This doesn't mean your whole life is on hold. Keep living your life, just let go of expectations.

Break Your Plans

What's your five-year plan? Ten year? How about your plans for next week? Put them away. The Wheel of Fortune has taken charge of your plans. Hold onto your basic goals, but give them some space to breathe. Gripping your plan too tightly could prevent you from seeing another possibility that The Wheel pushes your way. Practice by breaking your routine on purpose. Change it up. And stop beating yourself up when you don't hit unrealistic goals you set out of guilt or fear.

Projection Spreads

The Wheel of Fortune promises a time of good luck and a broadening outlook. Expect the unexpected. Take on an attitude of unapologetic optimism. If something doesn't work out, it wasn't meant to be, at least not right now. If you can appreciate the moment you are in as a stroke of luck, you won't get frustrated if plans are delayed.

Love and Relationships

If you are looking for love, the Universe is on your side. The wheels are turning. It may not be your time now, but it will be your time. While you wait, fill the time by revisiting what you want in a relationship and in life. Sometimes our love aspirations don't update to match our life aspirations. Make sure they are in alignment so you are ready when The Wheel spins your way.

If you are in a relationship, expect some growth. It may be quiet, but it will improve your relationship in the long run.

Career and Money

The Wheel of Fortune takes away your control. This can be especially frustrating in matters of money and career. There is nothing for you to do. Keep your head down, stay hopeful, and say yes to any opportunities that arise no matter how insignificant they seem. They could grow into something big.

Challenge/Reversal

There are times when The Wheel of Fortune feels like a massive roadblock. The Universe does not have the concept of time that we have. You may wait an uncomfortably long time for your situation to move forward.

X THE WHEEL OF FORTUNE

X

The Wheel of Fortune

Astrological Association

Jupiter is the planet of luck, expansion, and good fortune.

Hebrew Letter: כ

The letter Kaph represents submission, the release of desire for control. It corresponds to the path on the Tree of Life connecting Chesed (mercy) and Netsach (victory).

Crystal

Peridot. Inspires optimism and enjoyment of life.

Apothecary

Nutmeg. Heightens extra-sensory perception and draws luck and prosperity.

Affirmation

I am exactly where and when I am supposed to be.

XI Justice

Justice teaches us to seek out and right any imbalances we see in ourselves and the world. From the small and mundane to the big and profound, imbalances have the power to weigh our hearts down. So read more novels, contribute to organizations that help others, wear comfortable shoes. There might be another place we go when we leave our bodies, but all we know for sure is we have a finite amount of time on this planet. Make your stay here light on your heart.

Don't Hate, Liberate

Justice works on a binary model. Too much work and not enough rest? Too many tears, not enough laughter? Too many salads, too few treats? Reverse the equation until both sides are equal. This means that when we see a deficiency or excess, we have to find its opposite in order to even it out. Sometimes it can be tempting to seek justice through the source of the imbalance. Remember, the opposite of oppression is not retribution, it is liberation.

XI JUSTICE

Justice

Projection Spreads

When Justice appears on your path, the Universe is helping you balance out some aspect of your life. You may get a choice in what that is, so do some thinking and mark out some time on your calendar for an adjustment period.

Love and Relationships

Whether you are looking for love or in a relationship, Justice indicates that you need to make some changes in order to make a welcome space for love. Make your own life as harmonious and balanced as possible before any situation with another person can move forward.

If you are single, your next relationship could be with someone who is different enough from your past partners to "balance out" your pattern.

If you are in a relationship, check in with your partner and yourself to make sure everything feels fair to both of you.

Career and Money

Justice can indicate a need to shift your mindset in money matters. Scarcity/abundance, saving/spending, and high/low risk investing are all possible topics to consider. Look at what your beliefs, feelings, and habits are and see what can be changed.

A career change is supported if you have been feeling weighed down at work. If you don't want to change jobs, look for ways your job can be fitted to your needs instead of vice versa.

Challenge/Reversal

There could be difficulty in achieving balance, a balance shift that is not in your favor, or a new imbalance. None of these are impossible to work through. Do what you can to navigate shifting circumstances and be extra good to yourself.

Astrological Association

Libra is represented by the scales of justice, the only sign to be symbolized by an object and not an animal or human figure.

Hebrew Letter: ל

The letter Lamed represents learning, information processed into understanding. It corresponds to the path on the Tree of Life connecting Chesed (mercy) and Geburah (severity).

Crystal

Tiger Eye. Clarifies vision, grounds the body, and balances energies.

Apothecary

Olive. Symbolizes peace and harmony.

Affirmation

I treat myself and others fairly.

XII The Hanged Man

The Hanged Man teaches us to see the world from a new perspective. Occasionally we stumble into a different world view from our own, but most of the time, we have to seek it out. Pull yourself out of your routine to help open your mind to larger ideas and concepts that will expand your thinking and encourage empathy and growth.

More Isn't Necessarily More

There are many ways to change your view of the world. If you have the desire and means, traveling to far-off places or engaging in mind-altering rituals can be wonderful options. But you can achieve the same results by sitting against a tree in a park and focusing your attention on the feeling of the bark against your back, the grass under your legs, the sun on your face.

Projection Spreads

The Hanged Man signals a need to pause and reevaluate where you are headed. There is something outside of your current field of vision that will have a major impact on the choices you make. Moving forward without doing the work to see the world differently will lead to frustration. Help the Universe help you. Bend over backward—literally if you have to—to get a different view of your situation.

Love and Relationships

In matters of the heart, The Hanged Man has more questions than answers.

If you're looking for love, ask yourself what you are looking for in a romantic partner and why, whether your methods match your goals, and what image you are projecting. Then ask a close friend if they think your answers hold water. There may be a significant portion of the dating pool you are cutting yourself off from without even knowing it.

If you are in a relationship, it's time to shake things up. Go on a weekend adventure to someplace you've never been, or simply try a new restaurant together. Engage in a way you haven't before. While you do, try to meet your partner again as if for the first time.

Career and Money

The Hanged Man offers excellent support for taking stock of your career and financial goals. If you've wanted to make a change, this is great news. If you are not interested in making a change, you will still need to evaluate your situation anew, or better yet, get an outside opinion from a financial advisor or ask a colleague to help you re-assess your skill set.

Self-employed people may see interest in their work from surprising places that cause them to see what they do (and what they charge) in a new light.

Challenge/Reversal

Sometimes our view from a new vantage point shows us something we don't want to see. You may be asked to consider some uncomfortable truths about yourself or your situation. Be thankful for the information and move forward as gracefully as you can.

XII THE HANGED MAN

XII

The Hanged Man

Astrological Association

Neptune is the dreamy mystic of the solar system.

Hebrew Letter: מ

The letter Mem represents emergence, the first steps into a new world. It corresponds to the path on the Tree of Life connecting Geburah (severity) and Hod (splendor).

Crystal

Lepidolite. Quiets the mind to ease worry.

Apothecary

Mushrooms. A gateway to the transformative power of the Earth.

Affirmation

I turn my gaze in an unfamiliar direction to gain a new perspective.

XIII Death

Death teaches us to let go of the fantasy of permanence and accept the temporal nature of life on Earth. In order for new life to emerge, space must be cleared by death. This is true in our ecosystem and also in our jobs, relationships, and homes. Mourn the loss of what was and then turn to welcome and celebrate what will soon be.

Don't Fear the Reaper

While Death is one of the most dreaded cards in the deck for those unfamiliar with tarot, it is truly a blessing in any reading. Death does not necessarily indicate an abrupt or total end. In most cases, there is something getting in the way of the evolution of a situation that needs to be released. Once this is done, a new blossoming can begin.

XIII DEATH

Death

Projection Spreads

When the Death card shows up on your path, you are headed into a time of transformation. You can prepare by reflecting on where and who you are in life now and how that may differ from the past. Consider what is most important to you and make peace with parting with whatever the Universe deems ready to go.

Love and Relationships

If you are looking for love, the Death card indicates a need to leave behind old habits of the heart. Depending on how deeply entrenched these are (and how problematic) you might accomplish this through journaling, talking with friends, or speaking with a counselor. What we expect and accept in romantic relationships is ingrained in us early in life. As adults, we can keep these patterns or work to make new choices.

If you are in a relationship, let old grudges die. Clear the score cards and move on. If you can't, it may be time to move on alone.

Career and Money

The Death card is more associated with internal psychic and emotional processes than with the material world. It could indicate a need to let your current way of dealing with work and money die so a new model can grow or it might be a call to overhaul your career, letting go of everything to get a fresh start. Look to the other cards in the spread and to your own intuition and practical needs for guidance on how to proceed.

Challenge/Reversal

A particularly difficult or prolonged departure may be in store. Be kind to yourself and remember that new days lie ahead.

Astrological Association

Scorpio is symbolized by both the scorpion and the eagle and associated with sex, death, and all things that reside in the dark corners of the psyche.

Hebrew Letter: נ

The letter Nun represents humility, the acceptance of the whole self. It corresponds to the path on the Tree of Life connecting Tiphareth (beauty) and Netsach (victory).

Crystal

Black Tourmaline. Wards off negative energies.

Apothecary

Myrrh. Assists in the crossing between the worlds of the dead and living.

Affirmation

I release all that is not mine.

XIV Temperance

Temperance teaches us the benefits of moderation. When you pull back on how much energy you are putting out, you can make purposeful decisions about where to spend that energy moving forward. If Justice calls for a two-dimensional balance, Temperance requires a three- or even four-dimensional leveling. This is a full life rebalancing. Do less, assess, progress.

Mind Your Peace and Virtues

Temperance gets its name from the personification of the Christian virtue. Temperance, a model of pious self-restraint, was one of the figures popular in the morality plays of 15th-century Southern Europe (the time the tarot deck settled into the 78 card system we know today).

In contemporary life, Temperance can be re-framed as the virtue of mindful management of one's precious time and energy. Focus your expenditure of attention and money on things that you believe in. Limit what you spend on things you don't. Your inner peace will thank you.

Projection Spreads

Temperance is a somewhat exciting card to see on your path. The need to pull in your energy implies that there is something you will need (and want) to use that energy for coming up. Look to the cards that come after Temperance in your spread or pull a clarification card for a hint of what that might be.

Love and Relationships

Whether you are looking for love or in a relationship, Temperance advises you to stop trying so hard. If things are going well, there is no need to push. If things are not going well, there is no need to try to force them. Yes, relationships can be a lot of work, but not for you right now. Rein in your effort.

Career and Money

In financial situations, Temperance urges a conservative approach. Avoid spending money you don't need to. Focus on saving. You may not know what yet, but it's for something big.

At work, put in the effort you need to, but don't overdo it. This is not a good time to try to prove yourself. Save your big moves for a time when they will be more appreciated. If you're looking to change jobs or careers, now is the time to save your extra effort for your next endeavor.

Challenge/Reversal

Temperance addresses not only how much of your energy you expend, but how much energy you consume from others. Limit your availability as a sympathetic listener. Avoid large gatherings. If substance abuse or dependency could be an issue, take a break from vices.

XIV TEMPERANCE

Astrological Association

Sagittarius is symbolized by a centaurian archer taking aim, a moment of calm focus in a storm of action.

Hebrew Letter: ס

The letter Samekh represents healing, the restoration of personal order. It corresponds to the path on the Tree of Life connecting Tiphareth (beauty) and Yesod (foundation).

Crystal

Scolecite. Lifts the mood and brings inner peace.

Apothecary

Sweet Violet. Promotes peace, protection, and spiritual connection.

Affirmation:

I spend my energy on my own terms.

XV The Devil

The Devil teaches us to find where we are limiting ourselves and to break free. Our greatest barriers often come from within. Fear, shame, and regret all seep into our beliefs about ourselves and our abilities and keep us from reaching our full potential. We can choose to live under the weight of self-suppression or we can wrest control from the devils of our own making and take our power back.

Playing the Victim

Helplessness can be seductive. It absolves us of responsibility and allows us to blame others for our difficulties. The Devil alerts us to areas we have power over that we are not exercising. This does not mean that our lives are free from actual limits or even oppression. It means that we do everything we can to live life to the fullest in spite of them.

XV THE DEVIL

The Devil

Projection Spreads

The Devil is rarely a welcome sight on the road ahead, but it is a promise of better things to come—if you make the effort to uncover and remove the limiting beliefs keeping you small. Clear some time from your schedule and do the work. If you're not sure where to start, pull a clarifying card for direction.

Love and Relationships

If you are looking for love, you are likely selling yourself short. You are capable and deserving of a healthy and fulfilling relationship. Do not get into anything serious right now. Think about what kind of person you would want your best friend to be with, then apply those standards to yourself.

If you are in a relationship, there is something that is preventing it from thriving. Before you cut ties, examine whether there is a solid foundation obscured by doubt or drama. You don't want to stay in something that is not good for you, and you don't want to walk away from something good that is going through a rough patch.

Career and Money

The Devil is actually a welcome sight in financial readings because it indicates there are bigger possibilities you just aren't able to see at the moment. Once you know that, you can actively work to clear your vision and claim your coins.

Challenge/Reversal

Negative and limiting beliefs can be so deeply embedded that they become invisible. This doesn't mean they are impossible to shake off, it just may take a little extra time and patience. Don't succumb to fear of the process and fight discouragement. If The Devil comes up it is because you are in a position to do something about it. You've got this.

Astrological Association

Capricorn is symbolized by the sea goat, agile and capable on land and sea.

Hebrew Letter: ע

The letter Ayin represents revelation, the truth exposed. It corresponds to the path on the Tree of Life connecting Tiphareth (beauty) and Hod (splendor).

Crystal

Optical Calcite. Provides insight into self-imposed constrictions.

Apothecary

Salt. The ultimate agent of clearing and protection.

Affirmation

I cut away the bindings of fear and doubt.

XVI The Tower

The Tower teaches us to break down long-standing beliefs that have solidified into false truths. The image of the tower, tall, looming, impenetrable, represents ideas and rules we believe are standard and unchangeable. When you shrug, sigh, and say, "that's just how it is," you've come up against a tower. When The Tower card visits, it's time to tear it down.

Swing the Wrecking Ball

Destruction is not always a bad thing. Many of the towers we've built or inherited are unhelpful and even damaging. Do you really want to keep believing that you are not allowed to call yourself a real artist? That you have to live your life just like your parents? That not wanting children makes you selfish? That wanting children makes you unambitious? Of course you don't. Throw that Tower card a welcome party and pick up a sledge hammer.

Projection Spreads

The Tower is disruptive. It does not care what is on your calendar. It does not care what your obligations are. Make contingency plans for everything and get as much done ahead of time as you can. If you know what it is in your life and/or psyche that needs to be demolished, let the Universe know. Prepare yourself, light a candle, however you connect best. And then wait for the lightning to strike.

Love and Relationships

The Tower is not an ideal card for a love spread. It promises dramatic revelations, sudden shifts in mood, and an overall unsettling dynamic.

If you are in a relationship, this is a make or break situation. Any wondering or doubt will be over soon and you will either know for sure that it is time to walk away or that you are in a solid relationship with lasting potential.

If you are looking for love, lay low and wait to see what insights The Tower brings to you.

Career and Money

Big changes in your situation or in your relationship to it are afoot. A job or career move could come up suddenly, by your will or against it. You may see long-held attitudes about money and work crumble before your eyes.

Put off any big expenditures until things settle out. If you have money tied up in high-risk situations, consider moving some of it to a more secure place.

If you have a history of difficulty with finance, the source of the trouble might be exposed and/or destroyed.

Challenge/Reversal

Information could be revealed that is particularly surprising or difficult to accept. Allow yourself to mourn the reality you thought you knew. Great change, especially when it is unforeseen, takes time to really sink in even when it is for the best.

XVI THE TOWER

The Tower

Astrological Association

Mars is named for the Roman god of war, but the planet's association with war deities goes back at least to ancient Sumer.

Hebrew Letter: פ

The letter Pe represents incantation, words moving mountains. It corresponds to the path on the Tree of Life connecting Netzach (victory) and Hod (splendor).

Crystal

Rainbow Obsidian. Helps clear trauma and shine a light into the deepest darkness.

Apothecary

Lavender. Settles the stomach, mind, and heart.

Affirmation

I trust the Universe to tear down what needs to be cleared.

XVII The Star

The Star teaches us that there is always hope. In the vastness of the universe, against all odds, we exist here on a planet with the exact right conditions for conscious life to form, traveling around a star on one of the swirling arms of our galaxy. A life force runs through our existence, eternal, unbroken, carrying us through the past to here and into the future tomorrow, guided by a shining star. Channel that force to make it visible for others.

A Public Service Announcement

Modeling hope and kindness can take many different forms. You might excel at speaking to a crowd, volunteering in a large group environment, or holding a friend's hand in silence while they cry. Find what works for you. Being of service shouldn't be draining, it should be fulfilling. Whatever you offer, offer it freely, happily, and without expectation. If you can't, find a different offering.

XVII THE STAR

The Star

Projection Spreads

The Star ushers in a time of promise. Dream big in terms of your development as a spiritual being having a human experience. You have more to offer the world than you can possibly imagine— and the world will return the favor. Consider how you contribute to the greater good. This is an excellent time to increase the impact of your good deeds.

Love and Relationships

The creative, nurturing, energy of The Star is excellent in love and romance. Be open, caring, unafraid. Vulnerability is the greatest strength in relationships.

If you are looking for love, be up front about who you are and what you are looking for in a partner. You are enough right here and now. You do not need to try to mold yourself into someone else's idea of perfection. The more open you can be, the easier it will be to attract a suitable partner.

If you are in a healthy relationship, you can take it to the next level spiritually. Lean into your shared altruistic love of serving your community.

Career and Money

Open up your mind and let your fantasies take flight. If you could spend your days doing anything in the world, what would it be? What would you do to support the common good? How much money do you need to live that way? How much to take the first step toward that life?

Get your ideals sorted out so you can set your priorities accordingly, then put your dreams into action.

Challenge/Reversal

If you are going through a hard time, it can be difficult to access hope for yourself, much less humanity as a whole. Take care of yourself first. You're doing a favor to the world. We all need you feeling safe and warm so we can work together to ease the pain of the world.

Astrological Association

Aquarius is an Air sign, symbolized by the water bearer, a person pouring out water to support life on earth.

Hebrew Letter: צ

The letter Tsade represents faith, trust without reason. It corresponds to the path on the Tree of Life connecting Netzach (victory) and Yesod (foundation).

Crystal

Kunzite. Connects the heart to the heavens.

Apothecary

Honey. Offers the promise of eternal sweetness.

Affirmation

I take my place in the eternal lineage of hope.

XVIII The Moon

The Moon teaches us to venture deep into the darkness to face our fears. Ease into it. Let your eyes adjust. Remove the threat of the unknown by acknowledging your fears and seeing them clearly. Your heart and your gut are here to guide you as you navigate through the demons of your past and toward the angels of your future.

Reflections on Reflecting

Taking a good hard look in the mirror at your subconscious can be difficult to accomplish. If your fears are subconscious, how do you know what they are? Start by looking at what you naturally avoid. Is it a simple preference or is there something more going on beneath the surface? Meditate on it, write about it, talk about it with someone who knows and loves you well. And be sure to keep a dream journal on your night stand. You never know what symbols will come bubbling up into your head at night.

Projection Spreads

The Moon is a leveling up card. Take advantage of this time to process as much as you are ready and able to. The fears you conquer will not haunt you again. Even if they try, they will have no power because you'll no longer be afraid. This is your time to seek out and slay your monster.

Love and Relationships

If you are looking for love, The Moon helps you see where you are holding back. In many cases, this is due to a fear of rejection. Consider what would be worse—being rejected for who you are and learning someone is definitely not right for you or missing out on someone who is right for you because you are too afraid to show them your true self.

If you are in a relationship, there is a lot of healing potential now. Have any difficult conversations you've been putting off. Broach taboo subjects. When you dare to dive into dark waters, you'll come back up refreshed and closer than ever.

Career and Money

The motivation for your financial choices is up for interrogation. If you tend to stick to steady employment and conservative expenditure, consider whether an aversion to risk has caused you to pass on potentially lucrative opportunities. Conversely, if you habitually jump from gig to gig, a fear of commitment may be keeping you from locking into a great long-term career. Unlock your potential by examining your habits.

Challenge/Reversal

The subconscious can be an unpleasant place to visit. Reflection on the roots of our phobias and aversions can bring up painful memories of events that bore them. If you are not in a good mindset or a place that feels safe, get yourself on more solid ground before you wade in.

XVIII THE MOON

XVIII

The Moon

Astrological Association

Pisces is the dreamy mystic of the zodiac, symbolized by two fish.

Hebrew Letter: ק

The letter Qoph represents transformation, personal revolution. It corresponds to the path on the Tree of Life connecting Netzach (victory) and Malkuth (kingdom).

Crystal

Iolite. Provides insight to heal old wounds.

Apothecary

Mint. Heightens extra-sensory perception.

Affirmation

I am stronger than my fears.

XIX The Sun

The Sun teaches us to open our eyes and accept the truth that lies before us. Stop looking for hidden meaning and motivations that support your desired outcome. Everything you need to know is out in the open. Once you make peace with what is, you can begin to grow what is possible under the warm light of The Sun.

Find Your Photosynthesis

Whatever The Sun reveals to you is key to your development. Transformation is unpredictable. You don't know exactly what you'll do or how you'll feel on the other side. You only know that you'll still be you. Follow the lead of The Sun. It eventually sets. Take advantage of its wisdom while it's here.

XIX THE SUN

The Sun

Projection Spreads

The Sun shines its light on what you need to see most at that time. Wherever it comes up, you can expect to get clarification on something that has seemed murky. Be ready to act on the information. The energy of The Sun stimulates growth. It is up to you to decide where to focus it.

Love and Relationships

Believe people when they tell you who they are. The behavior you see is the only behavior that is on offer. Expecting something different will only lead to frustration and heartbreak. Pay close attention to the alignment of the words and actions of people. If they don't line up, give the situation some distance.

For those in a relationship, this is an excellent opportunity to strengthen your unconditional love for your partner. See and accept them exactly as they are.

Career and Money

The presence of The Sun suggests excellent growth potential in financial matters. Keep your eyes open and your feet on the ground. Make practical decisions based on facts, not wishes.

You could receive a lot of attention for your work. Speak up about what you want and if it isn't available in your current situation, don't be afraid to look for greener pastures.

Challenge/Reversal

When we get really set on an idea it can be hard to let it go, even when it is proven to be false. The simplest explanation is usually right. If something isn't good for you, let it go and move on. It is better to know now. If you have trouble distinguishing between messages, make a list of things about the situation that make you feel good and one of things that make you feel bad. See which one is longer.

Astrological Association

The Sun is the source that powers all life on earth.

Hebrew Letter: ר

The letter Resh represents reception, the decision to open. It corresponds to the path on the Tree of Life connecting Hod (splendor) and Yesod (foundation).

Crystal

Citrine. Lights up creativity, optimism, and sense of self.

Apothecary

Lemon. Clears vision and promotes longevity.

Affirmation

I open my eyes and my heart to the light of truth.

XX Judgment

Judgment teaches us to pull up the relics of our past so we can sort out the treasure from the trash. With time, memories merge and distort. We form associations with events, people, and places that paint everything around them in the same broad strokes. Nuance is lost. It is time to get it back by digging up the pieces of your story and putting them back together in a way that makes sense to you now.

The Good, the Bad, and the Ugly

While we use the word judgmental to refer to the giving of harsh criticism, there is nothing inherently bad about judgment itself. Judgment is the gift of discernment. We use it all of the time to decide whether it is safe to cross the street, what jacket to wear for the temperature, and if the milk is still good to drink. Think of judgment as a process of determining if something is good for you rather than if it is good or bad.

Projection Spreads

When you see Judgment approaching, start clearing clutter now. Begin with the most obvious—your closet, junk drawer, or a table that seems to collect everything. That spirit will take hold and open up more interior spaces in your heart and mind.

Love and Relationships

There is some old stuff getting in the way of your current relationship development. Look to past relationships for any unresolved feelings. Challenge yourself to find the good, even if it is simply finding the strength to leave. We learn valuable lessons about ourselves in every relationship. Discovering them can help you approach current and future relationships with more confidence and compassion.

If you are in a relationship, be open with your partner about your need for some space to process.

Career and Money

Buried treasure awaits you if you put in the work to find it. Clean up and organize your money. Follow up on invoices, double check your bank account for double charges, take advantage of any balance transfers or interest rate changes that could save you money.

At work, set a goal of where you want to be one year from now and start clearing out anything that does not help to pave that path.

Challenge/Reversal

We all have parts of our past that we'd rather not revisit. You could come up against one of yours at this time. Tread lightly and listen to your gut. If you feel safe to get into it, forge ahead. If not, see if there is something else related that you can dig into.

XX JUDGMENT

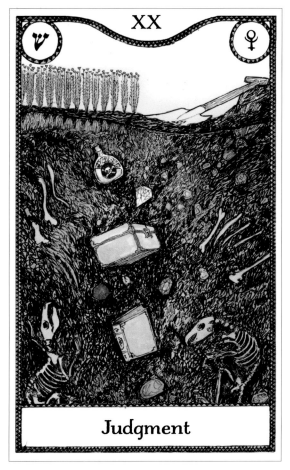

XX

Judgment

Astrological Association

Pluto is the agent of revolution and transformation.

Hebrew Letter: ש

The letter Shin represents revolution, triumph of the determined. It corresponds to the path on the Tree of Life connecting Hod (splendor) and Malkuth (kingdom).

Crystal

Fluorite. Clears and sharpens the mind.

Apothecary

Clove. Clears away heavy energies.

Affirmation

I determine my priorities and needs.

XXI The World

The World teaches us to celebrate the completion of one era and the dawning of the next. The phases of our lives don't have clean lines dividing them. There are interstitial periods when the elements of life loosen and rearrange themselves into a form that will best support the life that awaits on the other side of the portal.

One Specific Aspect

When you enter a portal, there is no way of knowing how long it will take to get to the other side. Life does not get put on hold in the space in between. You've got to find a balance between sticking to what you're doing and allowing it to transform while you do. Give yourself some sort of stability—a daily walk, favorite meal, time with friends—anything that reminds you that though your life is going through a revolution, you are still you.

XXI THE WORLD

The World

Projection Spreads

You are headed toward a major life transition. Even if this comes as a shock, it is grounds for celebration. You are graduating from this portion of your life. You have accomplished what you needed to in this stage. You are ready to progress. Trust the Universe to take you where you are meant to be.

Love and Relationships

If you are in a relationship, it is entering a new chapter. You may not be able to see exactly what this will look like. Don't let fear of an unknown future make you grasp onto the ways of the past. However your partnership is changing, it is for the best for you, your partner, and the relationship.

    If you are looking for love, your search is evolving. You may surprise yourself with a rapid revision of what you are looking for or in your methods of meeting people. Keep your nearest and dearest informed on your new thinking so they can help you in your search.

Career and Money

You've accomplished all you can with your current work or employment. Moving forward, you may feel like you are starting all over when you are actually starting another level of your career or financial development. Some things will get cleared out to make room for this new elevated era. This is good. Celebrate what you've accomplished and recalibrate for the next phase.

Challenge/Reversal

Being on the cusp of major change can be disorienting and frightening. If you try to control the process, these feelings will only grow. Let the Universe do its job. Float with the current, don't swim against it.

Astrological Association

Saturn is the planet of contraction, the taskmaster of the solar system.

Hebrew Letter: ת

The letter Tav (Taw) represents truth, what was, what is, and what will be. It corresponds to the path on the Tree of Life connecting Yesod (foundation) and Malkuth (kingdom).

Crystal

Amethyst. Purifies and protects the spirit.

Apothecary

Angelica. Removes energetic blockages.

Affirmation

I celebrate who I am and who I am becoming.

CHAPTER 5

Minor Arcana—Swords

The suit of Swords corresponds to Elemental Air, the realm of intellect and communication. These cards support rational thinking and guidance on how to analyze your situation and how communication, sent or received, may be affecting the energy. Most of us naturally lean on Swords energy to solve problems. We like to think issues out, to solve them like a puzzle. The Swords encourage this and offer a variety of ways to view life and to talk about it, and to identify and name what troubles you and why.

CRYSTAL ASSOCIATIONS

Aquamarine Facilitates clear thinking.
Lapis Lazuli Opens inner vision and insight.
Blue Lace Agate Boosts confidence in communication.

APOTHECARY ASSOCIATIONS

Mint Promotes understanding.
Dill Sharpens intellect.
Pecan Clarifies internal and external messages.

Ace of Swords

The Pure Power of Elemental Air

The Ace of Swords brings the gift of Divine reason. Clarity cuts through the fog of confusion, letting the light of truth flood in. You are a conduit for this truth, it flows through you and out into the world, shining on those around you, illuminating messages that need to be seen and heard. Fortunately, this card offers clarity in communication as well as vision.

Seeing and speaking the truth takes courage. Give yourself the time and space you need to capture the information coming in. Journal, talk to yourself, lie on your back and stare at the sky, watching your thoughts swirl around in your head. If you don't immediately have the time and space to interpret and analyze it, at least you'll have it all preserved for when you do.

In any area of life, you are invited to accept what you see and express what you think about it. Your eloquence will allow even tough subjects to be delivered and received with grace and love.

ACE OF SWORDS

TWO OF SWORDS

Two of Swords

Initial Wisdom of Elemental Air

It's decision time. You may not have all of the information, but you have enough to reach a yes or a no. The Two of Swords asks you to take the first step in taking control of your path. Decisiveness can feel like bad manners when you're not used to calling the shots. Remember that clarity is kindness. A clear no, even if it's disappointing, is much easier to understand and respond to than a muddy maybe.

If it seems like you are facing multiple decisions, look for how they are connected. Chances are good they are all feeding into one large decision.

In love matters, this card asks you to take the lead instead of waiting for someone else to make a choice for you. Depending on your situation, this can lead to a strengthening or a dismantling of a relationship. Either will be in your best interest.

For work and career readings, consider carefully what you want to achieve and then look for something you can say no to to clear the way for your progress.

THREE OF SWORDS

Three of Swords
Collaboration in Elemental Air

While conversations involving multiple points of view are the most interesting, they also have the most potential for conflict and misunderstanding. Facts are facts, but we all have our own truth, formed by our life experience and beliefs. When you feel yourself getting upset in discussions, try to think about how your own experience forms your point of view to have compassion for views different from your own.

Let go of the need to be right. Sometimes there is no right and wrong. Versions of events that contradict each other can be equally true for the people who experience them. Memory is emotional. Different details stick for different people and carry different symbolic meanings.

When achieving consensus is difficult it means all parties care. That is a good thing. Conflict is a natural part of human interaction. This is an opportunity to practice engaging in it in a healthy way.

Four of Swords
Stability in Elemental Air

Values and priorities that have been shifting are now settling into place. Your mind is at peace. Our values help us define who we are. You can see more clearly now what you are meant to give to the world, what message to send with your words and actions.

The Four of Swords indicates a need to check in with your own ethical standards to determine how to move forward in the situation. In love readings, it can also speak to a shared morality or a mutual understanding depending on the question asked, placement in the spread, and other cards present. In career spreads, consider this the foundation of future negotiations.

If you have trouble knowing exactly what your values are, give yourself quiet solitude to reflect. Meditate on it. Take a walk in the woods and listen to the songs of the birds and the wind in the trees. The information is there for you to discover.

FOUR OF SWORDS

Five of Swords
Chaos of Elemental Air

A nervous energy permeates every part of your life. Your words sound too sharp when they come out. Or not sharp enough. General confusion leaves you unable to make decisions or ask for what you need. The good news is, nothing is broken. This is a temporary state.

Think of this like your own personal Mercury Retrograde (the periods when Mercury appears to travel backward on its orbit, widely regarded by astrologers to be a time of crossed wires and miscommunications), but without the payoff of resolution. If you can, put off important decisions and conversations until this energy passes. Try to be calm in the eye of the storm.

In any situation, it is difficult if not impossible to assess the circumstances accurately under the influence of the Five of Swords. Romantic relationships can suffer greatly if fears and suspicions are acted on. If you are in a relationship, wait it out and keep the peace. If you are looking for love, take a break to care for yourself. At work, maintain the status quo until a more favorable energy enters the scene.

FIVE OF SWORDS

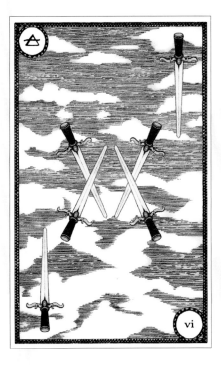

SIX OF SWORDS

Six of Swords

Achievement in Elemental Air

You have solved problems with your sharp intellect in the past and you will again. Remind yourself of your previous mental victories. Take pride, revel in them. All your past successes are present with you today, contributing to your current mental acuity.

If there are any issues you've had difficulty understanding, go back over them now. You have a heightened ability to untangle the most knotted strings of thought.

Address any ongoing disagreements. Take care to choose your words carefully, noting what has and has not worked in the past. A resolution is likely. If you can't reach agreement, at least you know that you tried at the top of your game.

At work, if you've been waiting for the right time to ask for a raise, promotion, or change in responsibilities, this is it. If you work for yourself, you can get your message out clearly.

Whether you are in a relationship or looking for love, state your needs openly. Your bonds will grow stronger with new understanding.

SEVEN OF SWORDS

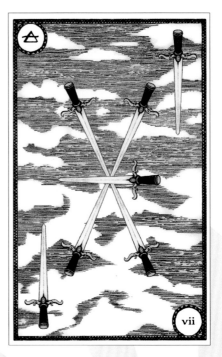

Seven of Swords

Overcoming Doubt in Elemental Air

The Seven of Swords is a portal to a new way of understanding the world. This new understanding is deeper and broader than you thought possible. There is nothing more you need to do to gain this insight than to simply acknowledge that you are capable of comprehending it. The wisdom has lived within you, waiting until you were ready to make its way into your consciousness.

You may find you speak more assuredly, trust your own voice, don't second guess yourself as much. This intellectual confidence puts others at ease. They sense they are in good, trustworthy hands when they speak with you. If you are an expert in your field, your career could get a bump. In any work, your ideas prove to be more workable and valuable than anticipated.

Deep conversations are likely to be revelatory and revolutionary. Spend time with those who matter most to you and tell them how much they mean to you.

Eight of Swords
Longevity in Elemental Air

Your paradigm of life has fully formed and will stay steady for the foreseeable future. This worldview is specific enough to create a workable system and flexible enough to remain relevant through life experience and broader cultural shifts. Take a tour and see if you have any lingering beliefs that no longer fit. If you find any, dig them out and let them go.

In romance, the Eight of Swords indicates a common language between partners. Communication flows easily and even wordlessly, both partners listen and are heard. If you are looking for love, your understanding of what you want in a relationship is fully developed. You can trust that what you look for in a partner now will work for you long term. If other cards are present that indicate the paradigm is not healthy, work it out before inviting anyone else into your life.

Career plans flow productively, setting you up for a time of ease and growth. If you are in a position that does not match your worldview, it may be time to make a change in your job or field.

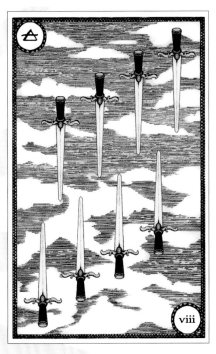

EIGHT OF SWORDS

Nine of Swords
Matured Wisdom of Elemental Air

Knowing a lot is great, but the wisest know what they don't know. The ability to see to the end of your knowledge allows you to push against that boundary and to marvel at the vast expanse of the Universe beyond that we may never comprehend. Your experience and study have brought you to this place. In your investigations and explorations you do not consume information, you engage with it.

Let your curiosity lead you further. See where your daydreams take you. Since you have integrated the basics, you can go wandering in your mind to find new avenues of inquiry. In relationships, this could lead to learning new things about your partner and seeing known information in a new way. At work, you can venture out of your comfort zone to acquire new skills. If you need help with finding a direction for this energy, look to the other cards in the spread or pull a clarifying card.

This influence is most enjoyable when it is shared, so try to find someone who shares your interest and knowledge level for discussions.

NINE OF SWORDS

TEN OF SWORDS

Ten of Swords

Exaltation of Elemental Air

You have officially thought of everything. For now, anyway. Give your brain a break. Take some deep breaths, relax, and look at all of the information you've gathered, evaluated, interpreted, and synthesized into your own unique viewpoint. Everything is here. If you still feel like you're missing something, walk away and come back to it later.

Accepting that all stones have been overturned is easy if you find what you wanted to find. When you don't, it becomes much more difficult. If you are facing information that is hard to take, give yourself time and space to process it. Disappointment is a form of grief and it has to run its course.

In love, the Ten of Swords signals that nothing has been left unsaid. The current situation will not be changed by talking. In business matters, this is a message that you have reached as far as you can in negotiations. It's time to decide whether to say yes or no. There is also a sense of being at the top of one's game at work, which is great for a while, but will grow stagnant if nothing further develops down the road.

PAGE OF SWORDS

Page of Swords
Earth of Air, the Novice of Communication

New ideas flow in like a breath of fresh air. Language pours out in unexpected ways, allowing you to see the world in a different light. The Page of Swords promises a transformation of yourself and your world simply by changing your words.

Language frames our reality. Our words carry resonance beyond their dictionary definitions. They reverberate through our consciousness, dictating emotional states and attitudes about our lives, relationships, and ourselves. Are you really bad at organizing or are you learning to sort your things according to your priorities? Are your relationships inherently difficult or are you working on your communication skills? Go back to basics to redefine your world in a way that empowers you.

Love, family, and work relationships all benefit from this energy. If you are in a partnership of any kind, identify the dynamics you want to rename and include your partner in the conversation. Words can lift you up or cut you down. You have the power to choose.

Knight of Swords
Fire of Air, the Champion of Communication

The Knight of Swords brings an unpredictable charge to communications. Everything feels urgent. The need to speak up and speak out is intense. This energy can be beneficial or detrimental to your cause depending on how it is handled. Organize your thoughts and practice saying them out loud before initiating discussions. Consider not only whether you are articulating your feelings accurately but also how you can frame them to be best received. No amount of refinement of your message will help it land if it provokes a defensive response.

Potential for volatility is high. Sudden outbursts are likely. Be aware of your emotional state and work to balance passion with reason to remain calm. If your temper flares in the middle of a conversation, be honest about it and excuse yourself until you can calm down. Words spoken in anger are great at punishing, but terrible at solving problems or promoting mutual understanding. Honor the value of your words by being mindful of how they are delivered.

KNIGHT OF SWORDS

Queen of Swords
Water of Air, the Nurturer of Communication

Your heart longs to be heard. Listen closely and let her speak. The Queen of Swords encourages emotional expression and understanding, both internal and external. Breakthroughs in long-standing confusing patterns are possible. Awkward conversations can be handled gracefully and with all parties maintaining their dignity.

This is diplomatic energy. If you see an opportunity to be a peacemaker in a conflict between people you love, this is the time to try.

While you may not achieve full reconciliation, no damage will be done and everyone will walk away with a greater appreciation for the positions of the other parties involved.

In love, you can be a leader in honesty and vulnerability, paving the way for healthy and happy interactions for years to come. At work, your colleagues will feel understood and cared for in your presence. You could be seen as a strong and compassionate leader and can act as an effective advocate for people or policy.

QUEEN OF SWORDS

KING OF SWORDS

King of Swords

Air of Air, the Strategist of Communication

The power of your visionary gaze could pierce steel. The King of Swords has an uncanny ability to assess plans and prepare for every contingency. However, thinking can outpace action, so be patient with getting to the results you see on the path ahead and use your voice and leadership to inspire, not criticize.

The calculated nature of this energy can be misread as aloof. When navigating emotional situations with the King of Swords, be sure to openly acknowledge the feelings of others and to assure them of your own personal investment. For committed relationships, this is an excellent time to plan for the future, especially your financial future.

For finance and career matters, this card urges big plans and decisive moves. This is a great time to launch a project, change fields, or reach for major advancement. Your ability to articulate exactly why you are the best person for the job is irresistible.

CHAPTER 6

Minor Arcana—Wands

The suit of Wands corresponds to Elemental Fire, the realm of action, intuition, instinct, creativity, and magick. These cards connect us to both our animal and spiritual natures, the parts of us that know without thinking and create without doing. Wands energy can be easy to feel but hard to find, so when it appears, run with it. As you engage with this energy, a connection and a trust will build with your elemental Fire within, making it easier for you trust your gut and manifest your reality.

CRYSTAL ASSOCIATIONS

Ruby Activates passion for life.
Orange Calcite Encourages open, playful creativity.
Nuummite Reveals and amplifies personal magick.

APOTHECARY ASSOCIATIONS

Paprika Promotes creativity.
Cayenne Stimulates vitality and drive.
Grapefruit Boosts energy and confidence.

Ace of Wands
The Pure Power of Elemental Fire

The Ace of Wands brings the gift of your intrinsic magick. We all have a magickal gift. Maybe you have a knack for being in the right place at the right time or an ability to make anyone feel at ease. Maybe you think of things before they happen or think of them and THEN they happen with no effort on your part. Whatever it is, the Universe is asking you to take it in your hand and direct it.

The Ace of Wands can act as a torch in a cave, illuminating secret mysteries that have been lying in wait to be discovered—unknown powers and unseen connections that hold the world together. You are a part of that system, which means that you too are connected to everything in the world by invisible threads that allow you to draw on the energies of the Universe.

In love, work, finance, family, anything—be careful what you wish for. You just might get it.

ACE OF WANDS

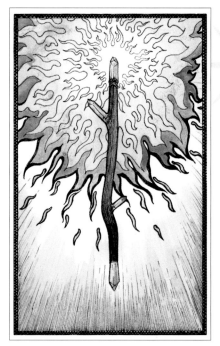

TWO OF WANDS

Two of Wands

Initial Wisdom of Elemental Fire

You sense you are being pulled away from something. There could be hesitation and uncertainty around this, a fear of the unknown. Work through it. Being pulled away from something means you are being pulled toward something else. You can't know exactly what that is right now, but you are being asked to take a leap of faith and follow your instinct.

In work or in creative endeavors, you could be branching off into a side project. The move won't require you to leave your previous work behind altogether. Not yet anyway. Feel your way through the transition without making any big decisions.

You could feel yourself leaning away from conventional wisdom in financial matters. Explore your options and do your homework. It is likely you are onto something.

Romance is not very well supported by this card. You need to be able to do what is best for you. Your actions may alienate someone if the relationship is not strong. If you are looking for love, wait until you see where this path takes you before inviting someone into your life.

THREE OF WANDS

Three of Wands

Collaboration in Elemental Fire

Creative collectives flourish under the influence of the Three of Wands. Your collective may consist of other people or it may be you working with previous versions of yourself, drawing on past experience to pave your own road to the future. Either way, innovative solutions light your way.

If you are in a relationship, you might find unconventional ways of connecting or cohabitating work better for you. Get creative and don't let traditional roles dictate your lifestyle. If you are looking for love, you may meet someone through unconventional means or in a place that you wouldn't normally go to. Pay attention to events you feel drawn to, and try to attend them.

At work and in your community, speak up when you see ways to address issues that others don't see. You may find there are others around you who have valuable skills that can raise the success of your plan to the next level.

Four of Wands
Stability in Elemental Fire

You've got to be nimble to stay steady on your feet. The ground may be constantly shifting, but you can achieve perfect stillness when you respond to changes in real time instead of fighting them. It's a delicate dance and one you are instinctively adept at. Turn off your brain and let your body take over. It knows what to do. Ultimately this is an exercise in letting go of control in order to gain more personal power in your life.

Shake things up in your routine. Take a spontaneous weekend trip, go to a new restaurant, work from the beach or the library. It may seem counterintuitive, but these deviations from routine will help your life and your relationships feel more stable and grounded.

At work, you may face a series of unwelcome surprises. Don't fight against them. There could be something extremely beneficial to your career hiding inside one of these unexpected changes to your responsibilities.

FOUR OF WANDS

Five of Wands
Chaos of Elemental Fire

Sit back, watch the action unfold around you, and try to relax. The Five of Wands cautions restraint. The internal voice you hear may not be your intuition talking. Instead it could be past trauma, fear, or internalized messaging from family or society. Making any moves could backfire.

While this energy can be frustrating, it's not really that bad. Sometimes the Universe forces us to rest when we won't take the initiative ourselves.

Sometimes we rush ahead too quickly and miss crossing paths with an important person or event in time. The directive to do nothing protects us from ourselves, from unintentional self-sabotage.

If you are in a relationship, sit tight. That funny feeling you have about your partner is either not fully formed or way off base. Wait until you have something concrete to talk through before engaging. If you are looking for love … don't. Just for now. You will be drawn to the wrong people for the wrong reasons.

Pull back from work duties. Put in the minimum effort. Any attempts to go above and beyond will go unseen or unappreciated.

FIVE OF WANDS

SIX OF WANDS

Six of Wands

Achievement in Elemental Fire

The Six of Wands offers a plan for powering up and taking action. Gather up all your magickal creations. These can be physical objects or photos, a written list, or memories of opportunities, relationships, and adventures you conjured. Relive the pride and satisfaction of bringing these creations into being. All of the magick you tapped into to make this happen still lives inside of you and is activated by being brought up to the surface of your consciousness, ready to follow the direction of your will.

Creative projects of any kind are very well supported by this energy. Career matters generally can be turned in your favor. Think outside the box and don't be afraid to push for a little extra. You'll find a good use for it.

This card brings excitement to romance whether you are dating or in a relationship. Follow up on any good connections you've allowed to fizzle out. There may still be a spark there. Long-term partnerships that have cooled can be revived.

Focus your energy on what you want to draw in, not what you want to get away from.

SEVEN OF WANDS

Seven of Wands

Overcoming Doubt in Elemental Fire

Your spells and rituals gain potency, your art reaches new heights, you barely get winded on a mountain hike. Signs are all around you that your elemental Fire burns brighter than ever. Believe them and set out to see how powerful you have become. Seek out situations and projects that test your limits. Staying within your comfort zone will not help you see what you are capable of.

You may have more gut feelings than usual. Take the time to notice their nuance, to learn how your body and your instinct communicate with you. A queasy stomach can signal nervousness or excitement. Recognizing which is which can make or break your ability to seize opportunities and your overall enjoyment of life.

Breakthroughs in relationships come through unspoken understanding. If you are looking for love, visualize your ideal partner often. They may walk into your life unexpectedly.

Work is what you make it. Really. You have great power to influence all aspects of your working life. If you want to launch a project or switch careers, this energy supports it.

Eight of Wands
Longevity in Elemental Fire

Your creative practice has hit cruising altitude. The energy you put out, the magick, your intuitive abilities and instincts are all finely honed to work together in sustainable harmony. Feel this pace, imprint it. This is the sweet spot of optimal creation without exhaustion.

If you are looking for love, this is a great time to find it. If someone doesn't fit easily into your life as it is now, it is unlikely they ever will. It is best to know now, so you make room for someone who will match your drive and appreciate your lifestyle. If you are in a relationship, it is hitting its stride in terms of passion. If that works for you, great. If not, it may be something to discuss.

Work/life balance is a priority. A short-term need for an extra push is fine, but it is important for you to care for yourself. Protect your time and energy.

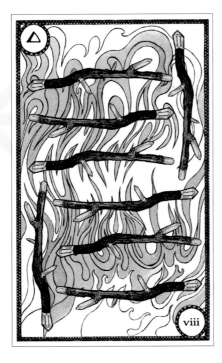

EIGHT OF WANDS

Nine of Wands
Matured Wisdom of Elemental Fire

You have become a master of your craft, and like all true masters, you continually stretch the limit of what is possible in your medium. Keep experimenting to keep your work vital and your creative brain elastic. This work contributes to a larger body of knowledge and experience.

Your magickal craft and intuitive abilities have also developed to a high level. No matter how skillful you are, always remember you are a human being interpreting the messages you receive and petitioning the universe and the elements to achieve results. There are many things that we can never know or experience while incarnated on this plane.

Romantic love is not of great concern under the influence of the Nine of Wands. In relationship readings, this card indicates an ability to trust your intuition and a strong reminder that not every gut feeling is truly intuition. Be honest with yourself about what you are sensing.

Creative work and careers thrive and grow. Finances require an instinctual approach.

NINE OF WANDS

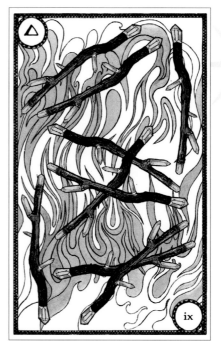

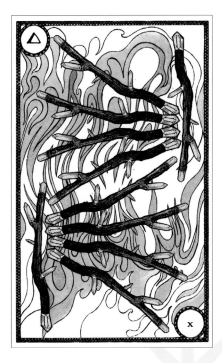

TEN OF WANDS

Ten of Wands
Exaltation of Elemental Fire

Your work here is done. All the energy you've put in has paid off and you can wind down your efforts. It is common to experience a bit of grief at the end of a big project. Try not to mistake it for disappointment. The Ten of Wands indicates the completion of a massive amount of highly skilled work. Trust in your abilities.

For work or career readings, this card suggests that you have accomplished all you can in your current situation and it may be time to move on. Look to other cards and your own intuition to tell you whether that means a departure or a new phase in the same place or field. Financial aspects are good, but with little growth potential.

In all romance reading, the same guidance is offered. If you are looking for love, do less. You are working too hard for it. If you are in a relationship, do less. You are working too hard for it. Take a step back and see how the effort you've put into your situation plays out.

PAGE OF WANDS

Page of Wands
Earth of Fire, the Novice of Creation

The playful curiosity that first tapped you into your creative center is back. Set aside the rules you've cultivated around your creativity and any limiting beliefs in the power of magick. Consider anything possible until you are proven wrong. There is a whole new world waiting for you to bring it into existence.

In career matters, the Page of Wands speaks to a fresh start with new skills. You can switch industries or move to a different aspect in your current one. The change of pace will be enjoyable, fulfilling, and fruitful. If you are an artist of any kind, this can be the start of a new era in your work.

Keep love and romance light and playful. This is not a time for tackling big issues in a partnership. It will only ruin the mood. If you are looking for love, keep your eye out for potential dates at impromptu gatherings and say yes to invites to cultural events.

Knight of Wands
Fire of Fire, the Champion of Creation

The Knight of Wands has an urgency and intensity unmatched by any card in the deck. This energy can feel erratic and even dangerous, but when managed properly it is a wonderful asset that can help you address long-standing issues and push incomplete tasks over the finish line. Refrain from confrontation and channel all this Fire into creation, not destruction.

If you are working on a big creative project, this is the ally you want by your side. (As I write this I have an orange candle burning with a Knight of Wands card on the altar in front of it.) Ask your brain to take a break and let your creative force take over.

The potential for burnout and exhaustion is high with this card. Be sure to take breaks from work. Set a timer if you need to. Drink plenty of water and feed your body healthy food.

In love, new romantic interests could be overwhelmed by your intensity and passion. Be mindful and respectful of their reaction to your energy. Long-term relationships can experience a renewal that has both parties spellbound if arguments are avoided.

KNIGHT OF WANDS

Queen of Wands
Water of Fire, the Nurturer of Creation

Your heart only wants you to spend energy on things you truly love. If you let it take control, you can conjure a life that is emotionally fulfilling and fun to live. Allow the will of your heart to flow through you into action. Move your body, put pen to paper, sing, explore nature, spend time with animals. Follow the impulse without judgment or analysis and see what you discover about yourself.

Work thrives in this energy if it is work you connect with emotionally. If your work does not, it will feel like a chore and a bore. Find something to engage with outside of work or consider switching jobs. If you have an established career, it will become very clear whether it is on track or needs some adjustment to be a good fit for you.

Your instinct for nurturing takes over, making you an excellent partner. Relationships flourish if this care is reciprocated. Pull yourself back if you are not getting what you need. If you are looking for love, keep an eye on any unhealthy patterns you have before you dive in.

QUEEN OF WANDS

KING OF WANDS

King of Wands

Air of Fire, the Strategist of Creation

The King of Wands combines playfulness and magick with visionary planning. Under this influence, your day-to-day life may lack structure and to others it can look like you are just winging it, but everything you do serves a larger purpose. Let yourself go with the flow. Your instinct knows things your conscious mind doesn't about what skills and experiences you need to reach your goals.

Leaders in creative fields can make great progress on projects as long as they have the trust of their teams. If you are not engaged in creative work, trust that the things you are drawn to now will help restore you so you can stay focused on your tasks.

Partners with a shared vision of the future benefit from spontaneous trips and dates to reconnect in the present. If you are dating, conversations about what you want in the future are important to have and can be handled in a lighthearted way. Even if you seem to have very different lives now, a similar vision can make a relationship worth pursuing.

CHAPTER 7

Minor Arcana—Cups

The suit of Cups corresponds to Elemental Water, the realm of emotion. These cards invite you to see your situation through the lens of the heart. They offer insight and guidance on how to approach your relationship with your world. Even the most pragmatic of questions has an emotional aspect. Whether your reading is about romance, work, personal development, or an upcoming event, the Cups encourage you to look into your heart to find the way forward.

CRYSTAL ASSOCIATIONS
Rose Quartz Opens the heart for love to flow freely.
Amazonite Assists in understanding emotions.
Ocean Jasper Promotes joy and relaxation.

APOTHECARY ASSOCIATIONS
Flaxseed Heals emotional wounds.
Marjoram Expands and strengthens love.
Avocado Balances the heart.

Ace of Cups
The Pure Power of Elemental Water

The Ace of Cups brings the gift of Divine love. There is nothing you need to do or say to make yourself worthy of love. You are loved completely and unconditionally, exactly as you are right now. Additionally, you are not only the recipient, but a conduit of this gift. Your presence creates a sense of peace in others, making life more enjoyable and more manageable for everyone.

This is not a call for you to love yourself (or anyone else). There is nothing active for you to do. The Ace of Cups encourages receptivity to the eternal force of love permeating everything in the Universe. In love readings, this can be a gentle reminder to avoid depending solely on earthly sources of love, an indication that the situation in question is looked on favorably (showered with love from beyond), or both. In career or money readings, turn your attention to your relationship with work and finance. This could be a fulfilling opportunity or you could need a reminder that there are more important things in life. Look to the surrounding cards in the reading and to the orientation of the card (upright or reversed) to gauge where the cards are pointing your focus.

ACE OF CUPS

TWO OF CUPS

Two of Cups
Initial Wisdom of Elemental Water

The Two of Cups represents the moment of attraction, recognizing a heart that beats in time with your own. Usually this indicates a new connection. However, that new connection can be in an existing relationship. When reading for love in particular, be sure to consider both the possibility of a new person entering the picture and of a renewed connection with a current partner. Look to surrounding cards for context and pull a clarifying card if needed.

In work, a newfound love of what you do, a potential business partner who feels like they really "get" you, or even a joint investment with a close friend could come up. Whatever the case, do not move forward unless you feel that emotional spark, no matter how good something looks on paper.

The spark of the Two of Cups is a lovely experience. Put in the work to stoke the spark to a flame if you want the connection to last.

THREE OF CUPS

Three of Cups
Collaboration in Elemental Water

Brew some tea and don't be afraid to spill it. The Three of Cups is an invitation to celebrate and talk openly with dear friends. Emotional support comes in many forms. Sometimes we need a shoulder to cry on and a friendly ear. Other times we need a distraction, a reminder that life exists beyond our immediate circumstances. Keep your social circle limited to people who

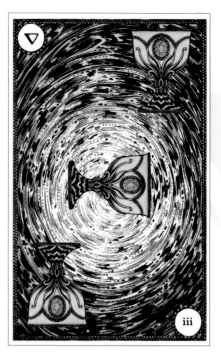

seem to know instinctively which you need. Let your confidantes know how much you appreciate them. Cheer them on, remind them how wonderful they are with your words and your actions. Let them see you smile and laugh. Conversely, listening with your whole heart to those who are nearest and dearest to you will open up opportunities for you to show how much you care.

In career readings, this card points to a need to share your desires with trusted colleagues. Opening up about your feelings around work and your goals will help others understand better how they can help. If you are unhappy in your field or position, your feelings are valid. Bounce ideas off of people who seem happy in their work and see what comes up.

Four of Cups
Stability in Elemental Water

The Four of Cups ushers in a time of grounding of the heart. New emotional priorities rise to the surface to form a foundation for growing current relationships and building new ones. Unhealthy or unproductive patterns can be seen clearly and moved away from. This is a reflective and restful, yet revolutionary energy. There is no need to run away from anything or anyone. Stay in place and pivot.

Financial matters are less stressful under the influence of this card, making any issues easier to solve. In a work reading, a different emotional approach is needed. There could be a source of stress that melts away when you reflect on what you truly care about—and what you don't.

In relationships, this could mean a new era of stability in an existing relationship or a need to step away from a relationship to attain stability. Either way, you will be at peace with the outcome and be able to love yourself the way you want to be loved by others. If you tend to have a "type," you can find clarity around whether that is working for you and why.

FOUR OF CUPS

Five of Cups
Chaos of Elemental Water

Emotions are separate from thoughts. While we explain emotions by tying them to a story (saying something makes us sad, for example), they can come up and take over independent of any instigating event. The Five of Cups is a signal that these independent emotions are flooding in and they are not likely to be pleasant. The important thing to remember is that they are not permanent. Help move them along by getting plenty of rest, eating green vegetables (they help with both physical and emotional heart health), and drinking lots of water.

No matter what subject your reading is on and where these feelings come from, don't fight them. Let them wash through, resist attaching them to current circumstances, and give yourself a little distance. You are not your emotions. Instead of saying "this makes me sad," try saying "this makes me feel sad" and see how that shifts your perspective.

This release is necessary. Embrace it. The storm will pass.

FIVE OF CUPS

SIX OF CUPS

Six of Cups
Achievement in Elemental Water

The Six of Cups is an invitation to take a stroll down memory lane, through all the love you gained and lost, through the work you did to mend your heart and come out the other side of grief, through the late nights spent listening to friends in need. Remember all the success you've had in emotional connection and growth. Let those successes buoy you now. You are ready to step into a new role.

In love readings, this card indicates an ability to get through a tough time with your partner, an opportunity for making the relationship stronger, or a need to remind yourself that you have navigated through stormy seas to safety and you can again.

For work or career readings, the Six of Cups asks you to take stock of what parts of your work have made you feel fulfilled, to look at where you've been to find out where you'd like to go next. In money matters, a sense of satisfaction is available with what you have right now.

SEVEN OF CUPS

Seven of Cups
Overcoming Doubt in Elemental Water

Dare to dream big. The Seven of Cups sends a message that your heart can hold more than you think it can. The things that seem to make everyone else happy may not make you happy. You have to uncage your heart's desire to find the truth of whether your current situation is or could be right for you. This card values potential. It is forward looking.

Fear of disappointment or failure leads to unexplored and unfulfilled desires. Push past your fear to pursue what you want. Your heart can take it. It is strong and capable of infinite expansion, just like the Universe that created it.

In relationships this means asking for what you need and leaving the door open for your partner to ask for what they need as well. If you are looking for love, look for the love you truly want, not the one you think is possible for now. The Seven of Cups in work and career readings calls for an evaluation of whether your work is adding to your life or merely contributing to your survival.

Eight of Cups
Longevity in Elemental Water

The Eight of Cups assures us that a state of loving peace is possible and available. While there will always be day-to-day ups and downs, you can count on a foundation of emotional fortitude built up over years and perhaps even lifetimes.

The steadiness you feel comes from within. Your emotional wellbeing is yours to manage. If there is anything disrupting your heart, take a step back. This does not mean cutting people out or confronting them about their behavior. This type of action only leads to more drama and less emotional stability. Take care of yourself and let go of the need to be understood.

In love readings, this card is an indication that there is potential for a strong and healthy dynamic. In order to achieve this potential, work out any ongoing sources of friction with a goal of making peace, not winning the fight.

In work and career spreads, the Eight of Cups speaks to long term fulfillment in the role, with co-workers, and with the work itself.

EIGHT OF CUPS

Nine of Cups
Matured Wisdom of Elemental Water

The Nine of Cups promises greater understanding of your emotional patterns, their source, and how to work with them instead of against them. However, this understanding will not drop out of the sky. You have to work for it. Even if you consider yourself well-versed in your heart's origin story and modus operandi, take time to look within. Your existing knowledge forms a platform that allows you to reach even further heights of emotional mastery.

This affective growth spurt is here to prepare you to engage with something important in your life more deeply than you are currently able to. There is something about the situation in question that allows for this opening and evolution.

In love, this new understanding could lead to a stronger relationship or it may come as a result of heartbreak. Look to the other cards in the spread for context. Either way, this is a gift. Embrace it.

In money matters, the Nine of Cups suggests that the situation isn't about finance as much as it is about personal growth. This doesn't mean financial success is out of reach, it just means that it is not the greatest win to be had.

NINE OF CUPS

TEN OF CUPS

Ten of Cups
Exaltation of Elemental Water

Raise a glass to the ones who are always there for you, who love you no matter what, the friends and family and community members who form your circle of support. Now raise a glass to yourself. You are a part of that thriving emotional ecosystem too.

Building a support system is a huge accomplishment. It takes trust and vulnerability, reflection and acceptance. That work is done for now. Rest, breathe, and revel in the love you've gathered around you.

If you are looking for love, get help from your community. Ask to be set up, go to social functions where you won't know everyone, be open to meeting new people through old friends. In relationships, you can expect to have the support of those around you.

Work and career opportunities come through personal connections, not necessarily from people in your field. If you are in need of financial help, do not be afraid to make it known. Those who care about you are likely to come together to find a solution.

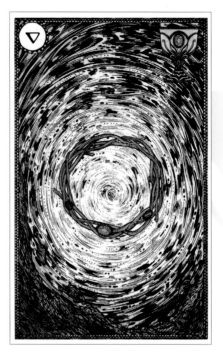

Page of Cups
Earth of Water, the Novice of Emotion

The Page of Cups offers your heart a fresh start. Old patterns and dynamics can be buried for good. New ways of feeling and expressing emotion are open for exploration. Most importantly, you can reset your relationship with yourself, loving yourself as you need to be loved now, accepting and appreciating who you have become.

PAGE OF CUPS

In any area of life you are reading for, you can expect to feel a weight lifted from your shoulders as you accept and appreciate your situation for what it is. The Page of Cups has an optimistic quality, always looking for the beauty in everyone and everything. Old relationships feel young, invigorated by an opportunity to "start again." New relationships can be judged on their own merit, not by the measuring stick of the past.

This is an especially supportive card in work readings for creatives. It suggests a renewed love for the work and the process that can lead to new artistic endeavors.

Knight of Cups
Fire of Water, the Champion of Emotion

The Knight of Cups urges you to wear your heart proudly on your sleeve. Whether your passionate devotion is to a person, a project, or a cause, you can't keep your feelings a secret under this influence. There is a protective quality to this card, and to protect something, you must step out in front of it, into the light.

Open displays of emotion emerge under the influence of the Knight of Cups. Welcome them. Suppressing your feelings will lead to inner turmoil and frustration that could burst through your calm facade when you least expect it.

New relationships can develop quickly, giving you an accelerated experience of intense bonding or burnout. If it's the latter, try to be glad to have the way cleared for a partner with the fuel to match your fire. Existing relationships have the potential to reignite a dimmed spark.

In a career reading, look to other cards to gauge whether any disconnect with your passion is something temporary that can be fixed with a small adjustment or a larger issue around a misalignment with your purpose.

KNIGHT OF CUPS

Queen of Cups
Water of Water, the Nurturer of Emotion

The Queen of Cups plunges you into a sea of emotion. There is no ability to separate yourself from your feelings or to control their flow through your body. You may have a hard time understanding where some of these feelings come from. That's okay. You don't need to understand, you simply need to allow.

Water and emotion are powerful forces that can show themselves as docile creatures or destructive behemoths. Both manifestations are needed for a healthy heart. If you feel like a tidal wave is coming down on you, you need the cleansing energy of this card. If you feel a lack of motivation, go with the flow. Rest and float for a bit.

Relationships can be difficult to navigate under this influence. Keep track of your feelings, write them down and analyze them later. If you are looking for love, it is likely you need to clear out some stagnant feelings before you can move forward.

If the Queen of Cups appears in a work reading, either immerse yourself completely in the work you love or take it as a message that work is not a big concern right now.

QUEEN OF CUPS

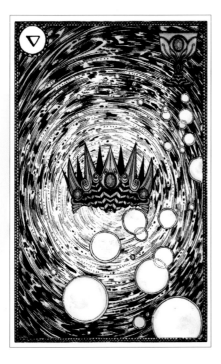

KING OF CUPS

King of Cups
Air of Water, the Strategist of Emotion

Feel yourself floating like a bubble up through the water of your emotions until you are floating on the surface. From here you can feel the waves, but are not overcome by them, no matter how big they get. You can see out to calmer waters and paddle your way there or be carried by the current.

The Kings of Cups allows you to observe your emotions and understand them intellectually. This is an excellent tool for strengthening all relationships in all areas of life. When you understand the language and messages of your heart, you can communicate your feelings to others clearly and accurately. This is an excellent tool for strengthening all relationships in all areas of life. Conflicts can be examined and resolved. You can hear what others are saying without reacting defensively.

You can use this energy to your advantage at work by determining what would make you feel more fulfilled and then advocating for your position.

CHAPTER 8

Minor Arcana—Coins

The suit of Coins corresponds to Elemental Earth, the realm of the body, home, finance, and all things in the material plane. These cards connect us to the world we live in. They remind us that we are spiritual beings having a human experience and that this human experience is sacred. The Coins bring the wisdom of the Universe down to Earth to manifest in the rituals of daily life. They draw our attention to the building blocks we use to assemble and maintain structure and stability.

CRYSTAL ASSOCIATIONS

Hematite Grounds the spirit in the body and powers manifestation.

Moss Agate Promotes stability and renewal.

Red Jasper Supports physical strength and wellness.

APOTHECARY ASSOCIATIONS

Potatoes Strengthen connection to the Earth.

Sarsaparilla Inspires healthy optimism.

Legumes Increase patience and growth.

Ace of Coins
The Pure Power of Elemental Earth

The Ace of Coins brings the gift of material potential. It is a golden seed that you can program with your own intentions and plant with the blessing of the Universe. Like any seed, this one will need to be tended to. When you are dreaming of what you want to grow, consider the time and energy you have available for this task. Set yourself up for success. Be realistic and specific.

Check in with your body. This is your primary Earthly home. If things aren't right between you and your body, every other aspect of your life will be impacted. Make any adjustments to your lifestyle you need to keep your body healthy. If this is a big overhaul for you, consider planting this seed for your physical wellbeing.

Career and finance possibilities are wide open. Plan for the greatest possible expression of your goals. The pace and level of growth will vary depending on other factors in your life, but the groundwork will be in place.

In love, exercise discernment. There is potential to put down roots for something real and lasting. Don't waste it on a situation that is not up to your standards.

ACE OF COINS

TWO OF COINS

Two of Coins

Initial Wisdom of Elemental Earth

Opportunities are taking shape. You are beginning to see what your world can become if you put in the effort. Enjoy this moment. Once you choose a direction to work toward, your range of options shrinks. Make sure you consider them all now.

This is your future origin story. The decisions you make now can set you up for long-term success or lead to frustration. Even small things can have major consequences, so be mindful about your choices. Slow and steady wins the race. This applies to your work pace as well.

Doing a little every day is great. You don't have to exhaust yourself. There is a long and satisfying road ahead.

At work, start putting the pieces in place for the next phase of your career. Take classes, research the field, practice your skills. You will be well prepared to take the leap when you get there. In love, you can lay or fortify the groundwork of a solid long-term relationship now. If you are single, hold potential partners to a standard your future self will thank you for.

THREE OF COINS

Three of Coins

Collaboration in Elemental Earth

The Three of Coins suggests that what you are building has grown outside the scope of what you can do alone. You need to find people with skills you do not have yourself to complete what you've started. Take a step back to see what areas of growth you have neglected or postponed, then identify what kind of help you need to move forward with them.

The best collaborations work when all parties are equally invested in a common goal. You may need to give up some control to make this work. If you do, make sure your trust is placed in good hands and draw up contracts where appropriate. When managed properly with open honest communication, your joint venture can thrive.

At work, ask for help when you need it and be honest about others' contributions to your work. Team or group projects are likely to be successful. Avoid isolating yourself or taking on too much responsibility personally.

If you are looking for love, make your search a group effort. Involve your friends and family (family of origin or chosen family). Trust in the group consensus. It may not match what you thought your ideal partner would be.

Four of Coins
Stability in Elemental Earth

A solid foundation supports you, allowing you a moment to rest. Your needs are well prioritized and accounted for. If there is anything you are holding on to that does not contribute to your situation, it will stick out like a sore thumb. Try to let go of it so you have more resources available for the things that matter most to you.

It can be tempting to remain in this place of security, but this is only the foundation. You need to look ahead to what you will build on top of this. There is no rush, but be careful not to let your situation grow stagnant before you make a move.

At work, you are recognized for your contributions and your skill set is known. Reinforce the good impression people have of you before asking for more or moving on. At home, you've built a life that serves your needs. This is the minimum you require to stay healthy physically, mentally, emotionally, and spiritually. Remember it and do not settle for less.

If you are in a relationship, it is on good ground. Consider what you would need to make it great. If you are looking for love, sort out your health and home life before inviting anyone into your heart.

FOUR OF COINS

Five of Coins
Chaos of Elemental Earth

Insecurity and fear permeate your perception of your available resources. Everywhere you look, all you can see is what you don't have. Focusing on what you lack sends you into a tailspin that is difficult to stop. It may feel as if your world is abandoning you. You need to ground yourself. Scan your body. Find one part of your body that feels good or neutral. Think about where you will lay your head tonight. Eat something. Establish that you are safe, right now, exactly as you are.

At work you may feel undercompensated, underappreciated, or both, even second-guessing your entire career. Do not jump ship. This energy is temporary. Once it passes, you can make a practical assessment of your situation. For now, stay the course. This goes for financial matters as well.

All matters of the heart should be paused. When you feel abandoned by the world, you are in no place to navigate relationships.

FIVE OF COINS

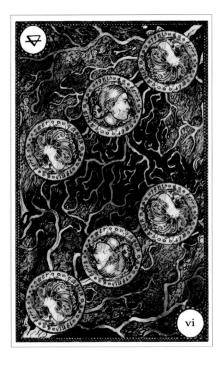

SIX OF COINS

Six of Coins

Achievement in Elemental Earth

You have a lot to be proud of and there is evidence to prove it. Look around you, at the work you've done, the home you made, this body that you've kept alive. All accomplishments that require care and dedication. The Six of Coins asks you to celebrate the life you've built, from the biggest wins to the smallest details.

In career and work readings, this card indicates a need to remind yourself of your history of success. Remember what you are good at and why. If you can, look at photos of projects or events related to your career high points. You are good at what you do. Own it.

If you are in a relationship, think about what makes it work. Living situation, routines, division of responsibilities, all the practical things that support a partnership. If you are looking for love, make sure you are acknowledging your own accomplishments so that you are drawing in appropriate partners.

SEVEN OF COINS

Seven of Coins

Overcoming Doubt in Elemental Earth

Don't dream it, be it. You have the skills to make it happen. You have not yet seen the full extent of your abilities. Keep building. You are making something bigger than you think you are. The Seven of Coins promises a high return on your investment.

Financial matters have great potential under this influence. Your money could grow in unexpected ways, you could get a surprise raise, or close on a big purchase at a good price. Don't overextend yourself, but do take risks that are appropriate for you.

Your career can get a big bump, especially if you make something tangible (material goods, food, art, buildings, etc.). Show how great you are through the quality of your work. It will speak for itself.

In relationships, this card indicates an opportunity to advance and solidify your connection.

Physical wellness plans started now have a good chance of sticking.

Eight of Coins
Longevity in Elemental Earth

Your productivity has reached its full potential. Your home life is stable, your relationship with your body is in good shape, and the work you do can support you into the future. Now you can fine tune your rituals to keep this system running smoothly with little effort on your part.

Put your bills on automatic payments. Schedule a monthly transfer to your savings. Sign up for a weekly food delivery or visit your local farmers market. Give yourself a bed time. Sticking to a regular schedule and automating as many tasks as you can gives you more time and energy to enjoy your life. We are only incarnated in these bodies on this plane for a short time. Spend time in nature, get a massage, bury your feet in the sand. Drink it in.

In love readings, the Eight of Coins favors the practical side of relationships. It indicates that things are stable, there isn't anything to talk about or work through. Those in long-term partnerships could check in with their counterpart to make sure that the systems they have in place for managing life together are still working well for both.

Work is great, don't worry about it. If you are bored, take on a hobby or side project.

EIGHT OF COINS

Nine of Coins
Matured Wisdom of Elemental Earth

Over your life, you have acquired many practical skills that helped you build the life you have today. It's time to acquire a few more. Take an inventory of your practical skills, then look for the gaps. Ask yourself what you would build if you could build anything. What do you need to know how to do to make that dream a reality?

Formal education is well supported by this card. If you have been thinking about going back to school, this is encouragement to do so.

Learning through apprenticeship is a great option as well, as is self-directed study and practice. Set a goal for learning and make a plan to achieve it.

Work can get interesting in a good way with challenging projects and problems to solve. Career growth is possible when you are open to treading into unfamiliar territory.

In love readings, the Nine of Coins encourages taking a class to meet someone with similar interests, or to strengthen an existing relationship with the shared experience.

NINE OF COINS

TEN OF COINS

Ten of Coins

Exaltation of Elemental Earth

Sit back and relax. Your work is done. Everyone is taken care of. The community you worked hard to create and support is ready to support you. Abundance is all around you. There are enough resources for everyone.

From here, there is only one place to go—back to basics. Start thinking now about what you will build next, what lessons you've learned and experience you've gained that will change how you approach your next project.

In work readings, the Ten of Coins suggests a plateau in your job or career. You can stay at this level as long as you like, but if you'd like to advance, you will need to start something new.

For questions around love and romance, look to your community for potential partners and relationship advice. If you are in a relationship, get out of your bubble and reconnect with friends you haven't seen in a while.

PAGE OF COINS

Page of Coins
Earth of Earth, the Novice of Formation

The Page of Coins coaxes your experimental side out. You are not afraid to fail and unbothered by the thought of other people not understanding what you do. New and unfamiliar materials and techniques attract you. You build with the joy and zeal of someone who has never been told there is a right and wrong way to make.

You are free to bring this spirit to your existing work or you can move to a new type of work or a new career. Artists and craftspeople are likely to try their hand at a new medium. Finances are helped by new and novel investments.

In love, you are invited to build a completely new kind of relationship, one you have never experienced before. Approach new and existing connections and partnerships with open-minded exploration. See what you can learn about life from the ones you love.

Knight of Coins
Fire of Earth, the Champion of Formation

The Knight of Coins reignites your passion for the world around you. You feel inspired to help build the ideal world you want to live in. Environmental concerns come to the forefront of your consciousness. Everywhere you look you see evidence of the magick of the natural world.

Your fervor affects all parts of your life. At home, you cannot tolerate anything that you don't love. Furnishings or decor that once seemed good enough may no longer make the cut. Your closet goes through a similar edit. Natural materials and fabrics will likely feel better to you both physically and emotionally. You may find it difficult to work in an uninspiring or wasteful environment. If you launch a new project, you will have the energy and dedication to keep it going.

In love readings, this card can indicate strong physical attraction. Do not confuse appreciation for the body with true compatibility.

KNIGHT OF COINS

Queen of Coins
Water of Earth, the Nurturer of Formation

You pour your heart out and a garden of wildflowers springs from the Earth. All around you, the results of your loving care can be seen growing and thriving. Your house is a home to all who enter and friends in need of support know they can come to you to feel safe and loved.

If you love your work, it will grow under this influence in quality and quantity, bringing you a great return on your investment. If you do not love your work, this is a good time to check in with your heart so see what kinds of things bring you contentment and consider planning a career change.

New and existing romance flourishes with the Queen of Coins present when there is a true love and appreciation there. Be careful not to fall into trying to fix someone you see potential in. Just because you think you can, it doesn't mean you should. Look for someone whose garden is as lush as your own.

QUEEN OF COINS

KING OF COINS

King of Coins

Air of Earth, the Strategist of Formation

The King of Coins has a dream of the future and the resources to get there. This combination of lofty vision and scrappy practicality makes for a high potential for success for any goal or project. Don't get bogged down in details. Know what you are building toward and get your hands in the dirt. There is something that can be accomplished right now that will move you closer.

New businesses, independent ventures, and hobbyists who dream of making their pastime their livelihood all have great potential for success. If you can, be your own boss. If you know you will need help to achieve your goals, wait until that time comes before taking on any partners or employees. Do what you can alone with what you have on hand. Think big and start small.

In love readings, this card asks whether the person or situation in question fits into your vision of your future. If you are in a relationship, share your dreams to confirm you are on the same page.

Index

Acknowledgments

Rohan Daniel Eason, thank you for being the greatest illustrator and greatest collaborator anyone could ever hope for. Your art brings this book and all our projects to vibrant life.

Jenny Dye, Kristine Pidkameny, Sally Powell, Geoff Borin, and the whole CICO team, thank you for your kindness, understanding, and patience as I coped with life and loss during this project. I am endlessly appreciative of the care and expertise you put into the organization and development of this book.

Anne Woodward, I am lucky to call you my manager and proud to call you my friend (and the reverse). Your wisdom and humor both ground and uplift me. Thank you for your excellent guidance and award show commentary.

Chris, my love, the Holmes to my Holm, no one believes in me more than you. You make my work possible and make my life magickal. Thank you.

Chevy and Gouda, my eternal Fool and Hierophant, thank you for coming down to Earth in perfect, tiny, fuzzy form to pass down your teachings to me. I hope I do you proud. See you on the rainbow bridge.